THE SECRET OF
THE COUP D'ÉTAT

PRINCE LOUIS NAPOLEON
(From a daguerreotype, c. 1850)

THE SECRET OF THE COUP D'ÉTAT

UNPUBLISHED CORRESPONDENCE OF
PRINCE LOUIS NAPOLEON, MM. DE MORNY,
DE FLAHAULT, AND OTHERS, 1848 TO 1852

EDITED WITH AN INTRODUCTION BY

THE EARL OF KERRY

AND A STUDY BY

PHILIP GUEDALLA

ILLUSTRATED

G. P. Putnam's Sons
New York & London
The Knickerbocker Press
1924

Made in the United States of America

"Dans les circonstances actuelles il faut nous tenir serrés avec l'Angleterre.   Les puissances cherchent à nous désunir— j'espère qu'elles n'y parviendront pas.

C'est là notre grande affaire, elle domine toutes les autres."

[TALLEYRAND TO FLAHAULT, JANUARY 2, 1831.]

CONTENTS

ILLUSTRATIONS

11

Illustrations

1851

By PHILIP GUEDALLA

I

THERE was a vague feeling in Paris that something was going to happen. Something, to be candid, was almost always happening in Paris. London might forget its fog in the blameless distraction of the Great Exhibition. But the clearer light of the broad and pleasant streets across the Channel seemed to provide an incitement to the larger, the more uproarious forms of political action, which public-spirited persons found almost irresistible. Had not the future of the human race been settled there, with impressive finality, at least four times in the last three years? First, the sudden disappearance of King Louis Philippe on a cold morning in 1848 had opened an almost infinite vista of felicity. Mankind, it seemed, was to be free. Then society, for the first time in its long career, had been saved, when General Cavaignac broke the *République sociale* on the June barricades and relieved the public

15

imagination from those apocalyptic visions of disaster, which crowd upon it when any threat is offered to the sacred institution of private property. So the citizen, it appeared, was to be left secure in the possession of his chattels. Once more mankind had watched respectfully, as a timid gentleman from London was installed as President of the Republic and took with him to the Elysée a heavy moustache, an unexpected profile, and the name of Bonaparte. The destinies of France were committed to a harmless magistrate on the American model; and the Republic, as he ruefully remarked, had found its Prince Albert. Then he, in his turn, had saved society by the happy device of sending cavalry to take a marching crowd in flank at a cross-roads on the *boulevards;* and once again the right of property was vindicated. But that had been in 1849. It was more than two years since any general principle had been established by the simple logic of street-fighting. And once more there was a vague feeling in Paris that something was going to happen.

Almost any one, oddly enough, could have told you what was going to happen. They would not all have told precisely the same story; but in each one of them there was to be a *coup d'état.* *On se battra,* as everybody said cheerfully, *dans la rue.* Some thought that it would be a *coup* by the Prince-President against his Parliament; and on dark nights anxious legislators patrolled the precincts of the Chamber in top-coats, to detect the fatal gleam of bayonets under the street lamps. Others believed that an indignant Chamber would arrest the unresisting President; General Changarnier was particularly vivid in his detail of the drooping prisoner's drive to Vincennes, and his pictorial touches were lovingly reported at the Elysée. A wider public lived in dread of a Socialist outbreak, with its threat to life, to morals, to property itself; the *Spectre rouge* began to walk again, and middle-class ears were strained to catch the first stirrings of the social revolution. Even the *Faubourg* took the strange infection; and it was whispered round Orleanist tea-tables that the Duc d'Aumale had gone to Italy for a purpose, and that the royal family were packing their trunks at Claremont. Something, it was very evident, was going to happen in Paris before the year was out.

But somehow it is never easy to associate the year 1851 with dark forebodings. For English minds that date carries a heavy freight of good intentions in Hyde Park. Mr. Thackeray was tuning the columns of the *Times* to unaccustomed music, with his dithyrambic discovery that

A blazing arch of lucid glass
Leaps like a fountain from the grass
To meet the sun!

His sovereign was receiving with unaffected surprise the intelligence that the architect of this miracle "rose from being a common gardener's boy"; and her Consort in the same season attended, with his customary verve, a *soirée* of the Institute of Civil Engineers, the opening of the Museum of Practical Geology, and a lecture by Professor Faraday. It seems a singularly inappropriate period for conspiracy; and there is something almost disarming in its sartorial oddities. One can hardly impute sinister designs to those sober gentlemen in vast top-hats; and how unlikely that their billowing companions in little bonnets should be the recipients of dreadful confidences. Yet fashion is frequently deceptive; and in black frock-coats and varnished boots, grasping umbrellas, Paris conspired.

There was the usual Cabinet crisis in October; and the President took a new Minister of War and brought a fresh Prefect of Police from the

18

provinces. General Saint-Arnaud looked military, and M. de Maupas looked important. But the new Government seemed less interesting than ever; and the world settled down uneasily to look for symptoms of disorder. It looked, with its usual courtesy, in the wrong direction; and whilst it scrutinised the politicians, it almost ceased to watch the President. That placid man had spent a quiet summer at St. Cloud. He had discussed a plan with some of his visitors; yielding to an old hobby of his, he had even drafted a few proclamations. It was now almost time to use them, and he began to fix a date. At first they inclined to November 20. Then the fixture was postponed until November 25. But something intervened. The President, who gave no reasons, adjourned it for another week; and the appointment stood for December 2. Something, at last, was really going to happen in Paris.

On the night before (it was a Monday) there was a party at the Élysée; and a little group slipped out by twos to meet in the President's study. The band was still playing at the reception, and they talked low. There was a brief rehearsal. Then, before eleven o'clock, the men parted. General Saint-Arnaud had his orders; M. de Maupas had his time-table; and the *coup* began. Paris lay out under the mist; M. de Morny was finishing his rubber at the Jockey Club; and the President had given orders to be called at five. Somewhere in the town armed policemen were watching printers rattle the proclamations off their machines; and the streets were quiet. In the darkness before dawn a battalion of infantry occupied the Chamber with a Cromwellian gesture, and M. de Maupas' officers were calling on the party-leaders with warrants for their arrest. Lights began to move in the Élysée, where the Prince was writing in his room. Sleepy Generals were roused by sudden orders; and as the day came up, the steady tramp of marching troops in the empty streets told Paris that something had happened.

There is a rare precision about the first movement of the *Deux-Décembre*, which it lacked in its later phases. There was a thin rain falling and the streets were full of soldiers with a proud determination to save society: the only difficulty was to find any one from whom to save it. The President clattered round the streets on horseback. But the proletariat obstinately refused to rise. Even the routed politicians did nothing more than indulge in a little mild sedition in an upper room and get themselves arrested. It was

discouraging for Perseus to find so little com-
petition for his Andromeda; but the saviours of
society proceeded firmly with its salvation. As
the light failed, a long line of heavy cavalry
came down the hill from the Arc de Triomphe
and trotted smartly round the *boulevards*. Fleury
rode in front; and behind him the street seemed
full of helmets, as the *Cuirassiers* went by. That
night the Prefect of Police, responsive to the
march of science, made free use of the new electric
fluid. He radiated telegraphic advice to his
Minister, to General Magnan, to the War Office;
and Paris slept.

Tuesday had been successful. Wednesday was
dull. A scared infantry patrol shot at a Deputy
on a barricade and killed him. But the loss
was hardly noticed for sixteen years, when the
poor gentleman posthumously became a saint
and martyr of the militant republicanism of the
late Empire. Towards nightfall some scattered
enthusiasts began to barricade the streets. Society
was menaced by a few erratic marksmen at upper
windows; republican exquisites in black coats
and yellow gloves deserted their favourite *cafés*
to gesticulate on heaps of paving-stones. To that
extent the monster had consented to oblige
Perseus with a perfunctory show of interest in

his lady; and the hero responded with an
immediate rescue. Society could, it must, be
saved; and on Thursday afternoon the impressive apparatus for its salvation came slowly into
motion. The Prefect of Police was still continuing
his impassioned solo on the telegraph, as the
troops marched out into Paris. The infantry
swung down the streets in the winter light; and
society stood on the sidewalk in its overcoats to
watch its saviours. A few scattered shots rang
out; and the men began to fire a little wildly.
There was a clank and scurry, as the batteries
unlimbered; and the dull crash of guns echoed
between the tall houses. The *fantassins* clambered
across the barricades with fixed bayonets; and
by five o'clock society was saved. Late at night
an anxious curator stood on the roof of the
Louvre and looked out across the city. The *coup
d'état* was over; and Paris lay silent in the moon-
light.

But its echoes were still in the air. "The
wonderful Electric Telegraph brought word" to
Mr. Greville; and London stared politely. The
Times was scandalised; *Punch* was deeply
shocked; and the Queen wrote a line to her
uncle at Brussels to ask what she should think
about it all. Lord Palmerston, with an indiscre-

tion happily rare among Foreign Secretaries, said
what he really thought and had to resign; and
Princess de Lieven rallied bravely to the winning
side. Slowly the echoes died away. Lord Palmerston returned to office; the Queen discovered
in her new *bon Frère* a respectable ally; and the
world went on again. But Paris never quite
forgot. The Second Empire came brightly on the
stage. But for the Emperor the *Deux-Décembre*
remained *un boulet que toute sa vie on traîne au
pied*. He dragged it for eighteen years; and at
the end he dragged it to Sedan.

II

A fortunate accident now permits us, after
seventy years, to examine a fresh witness upon
these familiar facts. His evidence is authentic,
and, unlike the vast majority of those depositions
which are patiently gathered for us by modern
historical science, it is really interesting. The
study of history lies in grave peril of being overwhelmed by the mass of its materials; and this
danger is appreciably increased by the prevailing
convention, under which no historian is felt to
be respectably employed, unless he is engaged in
disinterring either the despatches of a nonentity
or the washing-books of a celebrity. We have

almost forgotten that the business of historians is, quite simply, to write history; and it is perhaps to be regretted that they have so frequently usurped the simpler functions of the curio-collector. It is a happy circumstance that, in the case of most periods more than half a century old, nine-tenths of the significant facts are to be found in printed books; and if the historian is to abandon himself to the pursuit of the remaining tenth (an amusing chase, which is frequently dignified with the solemn name of Research), either he will not find it, or, when found, he will give to it a prominence out of all proportion to its true value. For historians, like other explorers, frequently exaggerate the importance of their own discoveries; and we are arriving gradually at a pained realisation that few things are less original than an original document.

But in the present instance a sponsor need feel no diffidence in the performance of his pleasant, though superfluous, duties. These papers afford new and valuable testimony by a credible witness upon events of general interest. The *coup d'état* was an event which deflected French history, and, by making possible the Second Empire, left a deep mark on the broader record of Europe. The work of those short

24

winter days in 1851 helped to free Italy and to
unite Germany; and its details possess a more
than anecdotic significance. Few observers can
have had a closer view of them than M. de
Flahault. He was in the inner circle of the
Élysée. He had been, in former years, the lover
of the President's mother; and he was the father
of her son, M. de Morny. So one can hardly
wonder that he was in the secret; and there is
every reason for publishing his papers. These,
by the happy chance that his daughter Emily
was Lord Lansdowne's mother, are in England,
and they tell a clear and connected story of 1851.

The *coup d'état* was not the first event in that
long and singular career, which unites two
countries and two centuries. He dated from the
distant, happy time before the Revolution. The
Swiss Guard still stood sentry at the Bastille,
and men were not yet brothers, when an amusing
Révérence named Talleyrand used to call on his
pretty mother. She had no children; and her
husband was middle-aged. So—with a bright
young wife, an elderly husband, and a gay
soutane—the child was born *en plein Crébillon*.
But as the slow stream of the Eighteenth Century
fell sharply into the rapids of the Revolution,
he was whirled past that placid scene in the

broken water. There was so much more now to
see and to do; and all his life long he retained
a queer capacity for being wherever something
particular was to be seen in Europe. At fifteen
he wrote a schoolboy letter to the First Consul,
overstating his age by twelve months and offering
to die, at any convenient opportunity, as his aide-
de-camp. This accession to the armed forces of
the Republic was transferred to General Dumas;
and the young gentleman was fitted out with
the canary-coloured finery of the First Consul's
personal escort. He sat his horse through the
long summer day at Marengo, when the smoke
hung over the vineyards and Desaix came up,
with the long shadows, from the south. For three
years the boy jingled on horseback behind Murat
and watched that fantastic silhouette, which
took the squadrons into action with a stage
costumier's hat and a riding-switch. He was in
the saddle at Ulm, when the beaten Austrians
marched out in the sunshine to pile their arms
before the Emperor; and at Friedland he rode
in one of those thundering charges, which threw
the Russians in the river and live in the tram-
pling rush of Meissonier's *1807*. After that, his
états de service follow the familiar career of the
First Empire across Europe. The names in 1808

are all Spanish; in 1809 they turn Austrian,
in 1812 the burden becomes a dismal Russian
refrain, that ended with the Beresina. Pro-
motion seemed to come easily—captain, colonel,
the Cross of the Legion, Baron of the Empire—
until he was a General at twenty-seven and
became an aide-de-camp of the Emperor, to see
the strangest sights of all. He rode with him
through the glorious *diminuendo* of the last
campaigns. One catches a glimpse of Flahault
reconnoitring outside Dresden with a cavalry
patrol; and once, during the campaign of France,
he was sent to negotiate an armistice, instructed
to tell a number of impressive untruths as to
his master's strength in the pleasing phrase, *Le
général Flahault doit avoir un langage honnête,
mais ferme.* But the game was up; the *vieux
de la Vieille* were falling back across France;
and the Marshals were beginning to mutter in
corners. One morning the Emperor dashed back
towards Paris in a post-chaise; Caulaincourt was
with him. Flahault rode in the next carriage
with Drouot the gunner; and Gourgaud and
Lefebvre drove behind. Three times in the day
they changed horses, and that night they met
the news on the road: Marmont had surrendered
Paris. There was a strange scene in the dark-

ness. The Emperor paced quickly up the road, stabbing his questions at a bewildered soldier— Paris—the Empress—the King of Rome—Joseph —the guns. Then he turned and volleyed invective at his absent generals. He would drive on to Paris; he would illuminate the town; he would sound the tocsin; he would call the people to arms; he would. . . . They were still walking up the road to Paris in the night; and beyond the river they could see a line of flickering fires, where the enemy had halted. Then Flahault was sent into the city to see Marmont, to stay his hand, to break off the treaty, if it were still possible. He pounded away in the darkness on a troop-horse; and the Emperor sat waiting over his maps. But Flahault was back at dawn with a note from the Marshal: Marmont had fallen back beyond Paris, because Paris would not fight, and the Emperor trailed off to Fontaine-bleau. Two days later Flahault stood at the head of the great double staircase and watched the Emperor inspecting troops in the court below. He looked a little wild and made a speech. The men marched off cheering, as the band in their tall bearskins clanged out the *Marseillaise.* He had another glimpse of him, just before the end. They spoke of Marmont, and the Emperor

COMTE DE FLAHAULT

Aet. 26 (From a portrait by Gérard, 1812)

asked, *Vous croyez qu'il me trahit?* Flahault
demurred, and the Emperor seemed to agree
with his reluctance to think evil of the Marshal:
Lui me trahir! c'est impossible; il me doit tout. . . .
But Marmont had achieved the impossible **and**
repaid the debt with Elba.

That was not the last that Flahault saw of
the Emperor. In the Hundred Days he seemed
to live closer to him than any other soldier.
First, he was sent on a wild peace-errand to
Vienna, to see Metternich, to make terms with
Europe, to bring back Marie Louise. But the
dove (its passports were not quite in order)
never got across Germany and returned to the
Ark. Next, during the hurried improvisation of
the last army of the Empire, he served his master
at the Ministry of War. Then he went north to
the frontier with Napoleon. He was with Ney
at Quatre Bras and rode back to headquarters
through the summer night. The Emperor was
half-dressed when he reported. In the morning
they rode across to Grouchy; and he heard his
master give an order—*Allons, Grouchy, pour-
suivez les Prussiens l'épée dans les reins*—which
lost a throne. The next day was a Sunday;
and the rain-clouds drifted over Hougomont.
They were a little late in the saddle: and the

staff sat watching the long surf of the French attacks break along the English front. In the afternoon Flahault was sent to order up the massed cavalry, which made the last charge of the Empire. That night he found the Emperor again. Darkness had fallen, and he was in an infantry square. Slowly they rode off the battle-field, as the Prussian horse went sabring through the night. The Emperor sat swaying in his saddle; sometimes he seemed to sleep, and Flahault held him. Once during the night they dismounted in a little wood near Quatre Bras: the Emperor's face was dreadful, and the tears came. Then they stumbled on towards the frontier. At Laon he seemed quite broken. But Flahault was sent back for news of the army; and the Emperor held on towards Paris.

In the last scene of all, when a fallen Emperor sat waiting at Malmaison for orders that never came, Flahault was still beside him. Perhaps it was natural, since the lady of that pitiable little home was Hortense; and Flahault had been, perhaps was still, Hortense's lover. One morning he was sent into Paris to argue with the Government: the Emperor was prepared to sail for America, if he might have the two cruisers which lay at Rochefort. There was a wrangle at the

Tuileries: Davout spoke insolently of his master, and Flahault in reply was coldly insulting. On the next day Napoleon's orders came from the Government. Joseph Bonaparte and Flahault were with him in the pillared library, when the two gentlemen from Paris were ushered in. They heard him consent to leave France. He was asking questions about the army, when a strange, familiar sound drifted in at the window. A column of infantry was passing the house, and as the men went by, there was a great roar of *Vive l'Empereur!* The man by the table seemed to pause. There was a map on it, and he leaned over to change the position of some pins with coloured heads. Then he looked up, rapped out a few words, and left the room. When he came down again, he was in full uniform. He would save France; he would command the army as a plain General; then he would leave for America *afin d'y accomplir ma destinée.* It was the last flicker of the dying fire. But word came back from Paris of a curt refusal: and that afternoon he prepared to go. This time he was dressed for a journey. But before he went, they left him alone in the sunny room where Josephine had died. He was muttering her name as he went in; and when he came out, they saw that he had been crying. Then he took Hortense in his arms and drove away.

So the *coup d'état* was not the first singular event that Flahault had seen. He could observe the nephew with an eye which had watched the uncle from close at hand; and that elegant *sabreur* of the First Empire survived to see the strange star of the Second Empire climb slowly up the sky, gleam brightly at the zenith, and then drop fitfully towards the horizon. The old man lived until 1870. All the world seemed to have died. The Emperor was dead, and all his Marshals; Hortense, whom he had loved, was dead, and their son Morny. Then, with an odd precision, Flahault died too on a September day in 1870, when the Prussian guns were opening upon Sedan.

III

Historical documents depend for their importance upon the volume of new light thrown by them on those controversies with which historians enliven the tedium of their narrative. The present collection, none of which has been printed before, will be found to possess a high technical value; since it contains fresh evidence upon several uncertain points of French and

English history. This unfortunately arrives too late for inclusion in the materials upon which my own study of *The Second Empire* and the more elaborate and happily still progressing series on the same subject by Mr. F. A. Simpson, of Trinity College, Cambridge, are founded. But it may perhaps be of service to append a few notes upon the extent and range of the new information, which is to be found in Flahault's papers.

This relates mainly to the following, amongst other topics:

1. Parentage of Napoleon III.

2. Orleanist plans for a *coup d'état* in 1851.

3. Flahault's complicity in Louis Napoleon's plans.

4. Louis Napoleon's occupations on the night of the *coup d'état*.

5. Casualties of the *coup d'état*.

6. Causes of Palmerston's resignation.

7. Conduct of Queen Victoria after the fall of Palmerston.

1. *Parentage of Napoleon III.*—The paternity of Louis Napoleon was long a favourite theme for disputation. Republican propaganda, during and after the Empire, luxuriated in indecorous suggestions; and well-informed persons are still apt to be incurably knowing on the subject.

This pleasing uncertainty has long been dispelled by researches, which are conveniently summarised by Mr. Simpson (*The Rise of Louis Napoleon*, 358); and it is almost conclusively established that Louis Napoleon was the son of his father, Louis Bonaparte, King of Holland. My own inference upon this point (*The Second Empire*, 43) was largely founded upon the inherent improbability that Hortense would be unfaithful to her husband during the dismal little Pyrenean honeymoon, which followed the death of their eldest child in 1807. This view is now confirmed, almost in terms, by a new letter (*infra*, p. 93) of Flahault himself, who may be assumed to be a reliable authority on the subject, since he was himself the father of her next child. His incidental reference to a story that Napoleon I. was the son of M. de Marbeuf is presumably intended as an additional instance of the scandalous untruths to which all prominent persons are exposed.

2. *Orleanist Plans for a Coup d'État in 1851.* —There is considerable evidence that Louis Napoleon's action in December was taken in order to anticipate a *coup* by the exiled royal family. Mr. Simpson (*Louis Napoleon and the Recovery of France*, 126) dismisses this story rather

summarily. But my own view (*The Second Empire*, 218) is strongly favourable to its acceptance. Lord Palmerston certainly still believed it in 1858 (ASHLEY, *Life of Viscount Palmerston, 1846–1865*, i. 287), and his evidence is peculiarly circumstantial. He appears to have been told in 1851 that the royal family were busy packing their luggage at Claremont and that an official emissary had offered to supply the *Morning Post* with full reports of a civil war, which the Prince de Joinville and the Duc d'Aumale were about to start in the north of France. Aumale undoubtedly left Naples about this time; and Joinville, after making a good deal of mystery about his movements, left Claremont for Ostend. Queen Victoria, although a most unwilling witness against her friends in exile, appears to support the story. At first (*Letters*, ii. 408, 413) she was frankly incredulous; but later she admitted (*Letters*, ii. 428) that "poor Joinville *had* some *mad* idea of going to France, which, fortunately, his illness prevented." Flahault's papers contain a strange corroboration of Palmerston's story. His memorandum of 1858 recalled a tale (slightly misread for transcription in *The Second Empire*) that the Princess de Joinville had been heard lamenting to the Portuguese Minister: *Et pour moi qui devoit être à*

THE SECRET OF THE COUP D'ÉTAT

Paris le 20! We have now a contemporary letter of Lady Palmerston (*infra*, p. 278) reporting in 1852 that the Princess had been heard to say: *Et moi qui croyais être à Paris le 20.* And there is in a further letter (*infra*, p. 247) an express statement by Flahault that Joinville had been provided with a Belgian passport "for his recent escapade." The fresh evidence appears to make it difficult to reject this fascinating story, which I had already accepted in *The Second Empire.*

3. *Flahault's Complicity in Louis Napoleon's Plans.*—It has hitherto been customary to assume that the circle with which the Prince-President shared the secret of the impending *coup d'état* was confined to Morny, Maupas, Saint-Arnaud, Persigny, and possibly Mocquard. There is a hint in the diary of the Austrian Ambassador (HÜBNER, *Neuf Ans de souvenirs*, i. 35) that Flahault was in the secret; and Charles Greville (*Journal, 1837–1852*, iii. 421) seems to have been under the same impression. But these passages appear to have been generally overlooked. The present correspondence, however, taken in conjunction with Flahault's presence in Paris and his residence with Morny in November, 1851, leaves no doubt that his name must now be added to the inner circle of the *coup d'état.*

4. *Louis Napoleon's Occupations on the Night of the Coup d'État.*—Nothing, so far as I am aware, has been known hitherto of the Prince-President's employment during the night of his great gamble. The dramatic imagination of M. Sacha Guitry once made a gallant attempt to fill the gap; but there is no authority for his agreeable conjecture. The Prince vanishes from sight, when the meeting in his study breaks up shortly before 11 P.M. on the night of December 1 (MAUPAS, *Mémoires*, i. 303), and reappears on the morning of the *Deux-Décembre.* A new letter (*infra*, p. 168) written in the early hours of December 2 and sent by him to Flahault now shows that part of the interval was spent at his desk; and it is pleasant to discover that Louis Napoleon personally issued the invitations to the strange cavalcade which followed him through the streets on the first morning of the *coup d'état.* It seems probable that this letter and the note to Morny, which apparently accompanied it, were written at some time after 5 A.M. He was called at that hour and he had expressed to Maupas (*Mémoires*, i. 237) an intention to address a similar invitation to the old King of Westphalia "on the morning of the *coup d'état*"; although the latter was never written (DU CASSE, *Les Dessous du Coup d'État*, 84).

5. *Casualties of the Coup d'État.*—Controversy has always centred round the casualties in the street-fighting of 1851. Whilst Bonapartists bravely minimised the number of the fallen, republican and Orleanist writers, anxious to shock French and foreign opinion, saw uniformly red, an unsatisfactory medium for the dispassionate survey of an arithmetical problem. The result is a grave uncertainty amongst all writers on the subject. Mr. Simpson (*Louis Napoleon and the Recovery of France*, 173) arrives at the conclusion that 1200 killed and wounded "may now be reasonably held to represent, not an exaggerated maximum, but a sober estimate of the casualties of the *coup d'état.*" It appears to be common ground that the military casualties numbered between 200 and 250. Mr. Simpson's figure for the civilian casualties is therefore approximately 1000. My own view (*The Second Empire*, 216) was far more modest and put the civil losses at "something more than one hundred and less than five hundred civilians." This opinion now appears to receive unexpected confirmation from a document in Flahault's papers. Most historians have been struck by the almost total absence of official information on the subject. Maupas (*Mémoires*, i. 508) reprints a Police report

of December 15, which estimates the civilian casualties as 175 killed and 115 wounded. But hitherto it has lacked further confirmation; and most writers have been driven to rely upon the unsatisfactory evidence afforded by stray conversations of interested people. There was a strange absence of papers on the subject amongst those found at the Tuileries in 1870. This omission is now partly explained by the fact that the original of Maupas' final report has been found among Flahault's papers (*infra*, p. 219). It had been sent to him in England during his unofficial mission after the *coup d'état*; and although he was instructed to use it in reply to anti-Bonapartist propaganda, the terms of the document appear to show that it was not produced for the purpose of publication. Its date (we have felt some uncertainty about the transcription) is December 25 or 29; and it estimates the civilian casualties as 215 killed and 119 wounded, a total which accords with my own estimate but is less than one-half of Mr. Simpson's. The natural increase in these figures over those reported on December 15 is accounted for by Police investigations in the intervening days and serves, in my judgment, to establish the *bona fides* of both reports. Upon any view of the facts, the new document must be recognised as an important piece of official evidence, which may well merit more consideration than the deliberate misstatements of hostile journalists or the hearsay of agitated diplomats.

6. *Causes of Palmerston's Resignation.*—This is hardly the place for a fresh summary of the complex of royal and ministerial exasperations which led to the dismissal of Lord Palmerston from the Foreign Office on account of his indiscreet avowal of sympathy with the *coup d'état.* But it is sufficient to call attention to the considerable number of new letters which refer to that explosion, especially to those gallant sheets (*infra*, p. 241 and p. 277) in which Lady Palmerston expressed "a Wife's opinion." And it would appear from the genuine indignation of Lord John Russell's "I cannot stand any more of these *tracasseries*" (*infra*, p. 199) that he was not quite a passive instrument in the busy hands at Windsor.

7. *Conduct of Queen Victoria after the Fall of Palmerston.*—There is an odd glimpse of the Crown in a new letter (*infra*, p. 273) from Lord John Russell to Flahault. It had always been supposed that Queen Victoria reached her zenith as a not too constitutional monarch after the

dismissal of Palmerston in 1851. So it is strange
to find her, within five weeks of that bright day,
compelled by her little Prime Minister to withdraw
a piece of discourtesy to the French Ambassador
and to substitute in writing the charming things
which she had omitted "from nervousness" to
say. One doubts, somehow, the nervousness.

But there is more, much more, in these papers
than one of those gaunt scaffoldings of fact upon
which alone it is possible to erect exact and vivid
history. One catches in them a faint murmur of
old voices across seventy years; of the Prince-
President speaking low behind his great moustache; of Morny, who was always bright, and
his Ambassadress with the golden hair; of solemn
English gentlemen in the Cabinet; and of
Flahault, who watched the sudden rise and the
slow fall of the two Empires.

INTRODUCTION

INTRODUCTION

THE contents of this volume are drawn, with a few exceptions, from papers which, on the death of my great-grandfather, the Comte de Flahault, passed into the hands of members of his family. Some of the original letters were written in French, others in English; but it seemed desirable, in spite of the disadvantages of translation, that the correspondence should be presented in one language. The subject-matter, it is true, deals with events which occurred in France, but the letters are mainly interesting as showing how those events were regarded in this country, and I have accordingly decided to publish the whole in English. The recent appearance of two notable works on the period covered by the correspondence served to confirm this decision. Mr. F. A. Simpson's *Louis Napoleon and the Recovery of France* and Mr. Philip Guedalla's *The Second Empire* have, as they so well deserve, been widely read by Englishmen; it seemed appropriate that such sidelights on the *coup d'état* as might be afforded by the discoveries of fresh correspondence, should be placed at the disposal of those who had already been enabled to make a closer acquaintance with Louis Napoleon as Prince-President through the medium of these publications.

Twelve months ago the Flahault papers had scarcely been put in order, much less perused in their entirety, and—in common with all who had written about the great conspiracy of 1851—Flahault's descendants were unaware how closely connected with it their ancestor had been. *The Second Empire* provided the stimulus for the exploration of these documents; its author has added to the obligation by the contribution of a foreword to this work, as well as by much useful advice in regard to its compilation.

At the time when this correspondence opens, Charles Auguste Comte de Flahault de la Billarderie was in his 64th year. His life had been full of incident, and his experiences varied. The Flahault family came of that old nobility so large a part of which disappeared during the throes of the French Revolution, and Charles

48

INTRODUCTION

François Comte de Flahault (the father of Charles Auguste) was himself one of its first victims. He was guillotined at Arras in October, 1792, on a charge which the Republicans frequently employed for the undoing of their political enemies —namely, the alleged possession of false *assignats*, as the paper money of the Republic was then called. Some ten years before his death he had married a young woman named Adèle Filleul, who, though she would appear from her portraits not to have been beautiful in the strict sense of the term, had beyond doubt great attraction for the opposite sex. But her union with Charles François Comte de Flahault was a marriage *de convenance*, for the bridegroom was already past 50 and the bride (whom before the wedding he had scarcely seen) was only 17, and fresh from the convent where she had been brought up. The relations between this somewhat ill-assorted pair were at no time happy, and no offspring came to bless their union. But if her elderly partner remained cold towards his young wife, there were others who were by no means insensible to her charms. She had not been long married before Talleyrand, at that time still in priestly orders, and soon to become Bishop of Autun, conceived a strong admiration for her. He was constantly at her side, while her husband was noticeable by his absence, and when at length the infant Charles made his appearance the obvious conclusions were drawn by those who knew the facts.

Though Talleyrand afterwards quarrelled with the lady whom he had once so ardently admired, he remained throughout the greater part of his life in the closest relations with her son. He may be said to have launched the boy on his career, for it was he who procured for him his first appointment under the Republic. Flahault's earlier letters to his mother show that the ex-bishop, as a Minister of State, continued to keep a watchful eye on the young man's interests, and that he constantly helped him by his advice and by his influence. Many of Talleyrand's letters to Flahault are still extant, and—though the famous diplomat was not usually demonstrative in the matter of his affections—the style in which these communications are couched would certainly suggest that the rumours of the relationship between the two were not without foundation.

A few months before her husband met his fate at the hands of the Revolutionaries, Madame de Flahault, with her infant son, had made her escape from Paris to London. She was assisted in this enterprise by Lord Wycombe, eldest son of the first Marquis of Lansdowne (better known as Lord Shelburne), whose acquaintance she had made some time before in Paris. Lord Lansdowne, who had a few years before lost his second wife, showed a lively interest in the young widow during her stay in England, and she soon made other new friends, some of whom were afterwards to stand Charles de Flahault in good stead. The boy was sent to school, and Madame de Flahault, finding herself almost without means, brought out the first of a series of romantic novels, which earned for her some money, as well as considerable repute as an authoress. But she appears to have been of a restless disposition, and early in 1794 went off to the Continent, her son being transferred from his English academy to one at Celle in Hanover.

During this period of emigration Madame de Flahault was in frequent correspondence with one of her earliest admirers—Gouverneur Morris, who had formerly held the post of United States Minister at Paris. It is from this source that we learn of a new friendship which was destined to have an important bearing on the later career of her son.

Louis Philippe, the young Duc d'Orléans, who

more than fifty years afterwards was destined to
fly from his country and his throne as plain "Mr.
Smith," had just escaped from the fury of the
first Revolution, and as "Monsieur Corbie" had
become a teacher of languages in Switzerland.
There he met Madame de Flahault, and it would
seem that these companions in misfortune found
each other's society eminently congenial. They
were some time together in Switzerland and
travelled in company through Germany to Altona.
"Mon cousin," as Madame de Flahault always
designated the Duc d'Orléans in her letters to
Morris, did not forget the heroine of this adven-
ture, or her son, and more than once during his
subsequent residence in England showed a kindly
interest in Charles de Flahault's affairs. Thus
when in 1830 by a fresh turn of fate "Monsieur
Corbie" found himself on the French throne,
Flahault was amongst the first to be welcomed
by the King of the French.

Madame de Flahault remained for three years
at Altona, where many of the French *émigrés* had
forgathered at this time. It was there that she
first met M. de Souza; but though the Portuguese
diplomat soon made her a proposal of marriage, it
was not till 1802 that she consented to take his name.

It was not easy during the earlier years of the

Republic for an *émigré* to get back to France; and it may be that it was through Talleyrand's intervention that in 1798 Madame de Flahault and her son effected their return. Charles was barely 14 years of age, but soon secured through his powerful sponsor a post in the *Dépôt général de la Marine.* Thenceforward his progress was rapid. He started his military service in the *Houssards Volontaires;* whence he was in 1800 transferred to the *5me Dragons*—a regiment then commanded by Louis Bonaparte, the First Consul's brother, with whom both Madame de Flahault and her son were on the best of terms. We next find Flahault acting in 1802 as aide-de-camp to Murat, with whom he remained for five years; but, as a result of some disagreement which Talleyrand unsuccessfully attempted to compose, the young officer was in 1807 forced to revert for a time to regimental duty in a distant part of the newly conquered Prussian territory. He was, however, not forgotten by his friends, and the next year finds him again an aide-de-camp, this time with General Berthier, Napoleon's Chief of the Staff. From this post it was a short step to Napoleon's side, and at the termination of the ill-fated Russian campaign of 1812, during which Flahault had on several occasions attracted the

Emperor's notice, he secured the coveted post of aide-de-camp to His Majesty. From his new master he would seem to have received a constantly increasing measure of trust, and during the course of Napoleon's campaigns he was frequently employed on special missions of a quasi-diplomatic character, in the conduct of which he appears to have earned considerable credit. He took part in all the principal engagements of the Grand Army, was often noticed for his bravery and was several times wounded.

The abdication of Napoleon in 1814 left him for the time being without occupation; like many others who had been supporters of the Imperial régime, he was compelled to make a virtue of necessity by accepting that by which it was replaced, and he continued under the first Restoration to live quietly in France. When ten months later the Emperor returned from Elba, Flahault was amongst the first to rejoin him, and he remained with him throughout the period of the Hundred Days. At Waterloo he was all day at the Emperor's side, and fled with him that night from the fatal field to Paris. He was with him again at Malmaison during the days which immediately preceded Napoleon's final surrender. Though not amongst those who were specifically

INTRODUCTION

proscribed by the new Government, he had little
to tempt him to remain in France, under a King
whom he felt unable to recognise. His movements were eventually determined by influences
rather domestic than political.

Some years before this Flahault had won the
affections of Hortense Beauharnais, the daughter
of the Empress Joséphine by her first marriage
and the wife of Napoleon's brother, Louis, King
of Holland. Though at the time their liaison
was suspected by a few, the story in its outline
eventually became common property; but the
unpublished correspondence of Madame de Souza
and her son supplies us with many details which
had been hitherto lacking. It is from this source
that we learn that the romance commenced much
earlier than has generally been supposed, and
that Hortense had been interesting herself on
Flahault's account long before she parted from
her husband.

It would seem that at the outset of this affair
Flahault, whose good looks and pleasant manners
had already secured for him considerable success
amongst the fair ladies of the Emperor's court,
was rather the pursued than the pursuer; but
however this may be, it is clear that he owed
much to Queen Hortense, and that he considered

himself bound to her, even before the birth of their son, Auguste de Morny. There is no doubt also that in 1814 he was prepared to marry her, but that she was unwilling to take the necessary preliminary of divorcing her husband; and from the tone of Flahault's letters, there would be reason to suppose that her affection for him had by then somewhat cooled.

But after the fall of Napoleon in 1815 the conditions were changed; Hortense was left without friends and without money, and in July of that year she was ordered to leave the country at a few days' notice. Flahault conceived it to be his duty to stand by her, and followed her hot-foot in her flight to her Swiss home. He was stopped at the frontier—Fouché's secret agents were on the watch and were determined that the sister-in-law and the ex-aide-de-camp of the prisoner of St. Helena should not be given the opportunity of plotting together against the Bourbon Government. For some weeks, accordingly, he was forced to remain at Lyons, under close surveillance, while his mother in Paris did her best to obtain permission for him to proceed on his journey; but all their efforts were vain, and it soon became apparent that the road to Switzerland was definitely barred. He was finally offered a passport to England; and to England he went in December, 1815, for the second time in his life a refugee.

He had already, as we have seen, some old acquaintances amongst those who had befriended his mother in that country more than twenty years before. He found there, too, friends of a more recent date. Lord and Lady Holland, who had been much in Paris during the Empire and made no secret of their sympathies with the fallen Emperor, received him with open arms. Within a week of his arrival we find him staying with them at Holland House, and his portrait still hangs on the walls of their famous residence. There was also Lord William Russell, brother to the Duke of Bedford and aide-de-camp to the Duke of Wellington, with whom (curiously enough) both Madame de Souza and her son were on the most friendly terms only a few months after the final defeat of Napoleon by Wellington at Waterloo. Lord William introduced Flahault to his numerous relatives and he soon became a welcome guest at Woburn Abbey, the Duke of Bedford's country seat. Lord and Lady Grey were also amongst his friends, and it was through them that he first became acquainted with the lady who was to be his partner in life.

THE SECRET OF THE COUP D'ÉTAT

Miss Margaret Mercer Elphinstone was the daughter of Admiral Lord Keith and heiress in her own right to Meikleour in Perthshire, a property which she had inherited from the Admiral's first wife, Miss Mercer. It is asserted by Mme. de Boigne that she deliberately started a flirtation with Flahault out of pique at the inattention of some former admirer, but that her affections soon became more deeply involved than she had expected or intended. The story may be taken for what it is worth, for Mme. de Boigne's family were notoriously hostile to the Flahaults; but the attachment was certainly not a one-sided one, and the difficulties which were placed in the way of their union required, before they could be surmounted, all the determination of both parties.

Lord Keith and most of his family were determined, if they could, to prevent the match.

Most of the Admiral's best years had been devoted to the frustration of the ex-Emperor's schemes; as Commander-in-Chief of the Channel Fleet, he had himself received Napoleon's surrender at Plymouth and despatched him under escort to St. Helena. It was therefore somewhat galling for him to see his favourite daughter joined in marriage to one who had been so closely associated with his famous adversary. The projected alliance, moreover, was viewed with scant favour in high places. Miss Elphinstone was a close friend of Princess Charlotte, heir-apparent to the English Crown, while from his previous associations Flahault was anything but *persona grata* to the Bourbons. The marriage seemed as undesirable to the British administration, which wished to keep on friendly terms with the restored dynasty, as it did to the representatives of that dynasty in London. The Regent made no secret of his disapproval, while the French Ambassador, M. d'Osmond, father of Mme. de Boigne (acting, we may suppose, under orders from Paris), lost no opportunity of damaging Flahault's reputation by spreading in London society all kinds of stories about his past life. There was a further difficulty in the matter of Flahault's religion, as well as in the question of his future status as a French citizen and officer.

But in the end and after many delays all these obstacles were somehow overcome, the marriage being privately celebrated at Edinburgh on June 19, 1817. Lord Keith for a time held no communication with his recalcitrant daughter, but this estrangement did not permanently endure. In a few years they had become completely reconciled, while the old Admiral had been so far won over by Flahault's charm of manner, as to consent to receive him in his house. Lord Keith died in 1823 and the Flahaults became the possessors of his estates, and of the house, Tully-allan Castle, near Kincardine-on-Forth, which he had spent his last years in building. The Napoleonic general thus found himself part owner of two residences beyond the Tweed. He added for a time the name of Mercer to that of Flahault de la Billarderie, and henceforward played, not without success, the part of a Scots Laird. There are still living, persons who are able to recall the affection with which "the Count" was spoken of by employees on his wife's estates.

In course of time no less than five daughters were born of the marriage—a fact which (as her letters show) their old grandmother in Paris viewed with unconcealed impatience; for she, no less than the parents, greatly wished to see a male heir to the Keith title and estates.

So long as the Bourbon dynasty remained in power, Flahault had neither the desire nor the opportunity to take a part in the affairs of his country. It was otherwise when the Revolution of July, 1830, called Louis Philippe to the throne. He was quickly on the scene and was at once well received by the new King. Important questions, in which all the great powers were involved, were then pending in the matter of the Belgian succession, and Flahault, who was a personal friend of the new Prime Minister, Lord Grey, seemed indicated as the representative of his country in England. It was, however, Talleyrand who received the appointment, and Flahault had to be content with a secondary rôle as an assistant in the negotiations which were then proceeding in London. But Talleyrand, then in his 76th year, appears to have conceived the idea that his protégé was endeavouring to oust him, and the quarrel was taken up by their womankind —Madame de Dino and Madame de Flahault. The intimacy which had so long existed between the two families was thus, for the time being, destroyed, nor was it ever completely restored.

Shortly afterwards, and probably at Talleyrand's suggestion, Flahault was removed to a new sphere. He was, in May, 1831, appointed ambassador-extraordinary in Berlin, but remained there only a few months. Two years later he became the *premier écuyer* to the young Duc d'Orléans, Louis Philippe's eldest son, a post which he continued to hold till 1838. In 1840, he went as French Ambassador to Vienna, where

he represented his country for the next seven
years. The Revolution of February, 1848, with
the consequent change of government, brought
him once more to England.

Madame de Flahault figures in this volume
mainly as the recipient of her husband's letters;
but it is clear that he was in all things much
guided by her influence. Miss Elphinstone's
mother had died while she was still an infant
in arms, and her father, by reason of his naval
calling, was at that time seldom at home. She
was thus much thrown on her own resources, and
early developed a strong individuality. Whilst
still a girl she had made the acquaintance of
the Regent's daughter, Princess Charlotte. She
soon became the close friend of the Princess, and
when this ill-fated lady refused to marry the
Prince of Orange, Miss Elphinstone was, however unwillingly, drawn into the quarrel which
followed between the Regent and his daughter.
Several hundred of the Princess's letters—sadly
misspelt, heavily underlined, and scrawled in an
almost illegible hand—as well as a large part of
the correspondence which she had with her
various royal relatives, remained in Miss Elphinstone's possession, in spite of several efforts made

INTRODUCTION

by the Regent to obtain possession of them. They are to-day amongst our family papers. There are also a number of letters to and from Lord Grey, the future Prime Minister of the Reform Bill, who through Miss Elphinstone (but unknown to the outside world) performed at this juncture the part of political adviser to the young Princess. With all this we are only now concerned as showing that Flahault's wife was, even before her marriage, ready to engage in other people's quarrels—as well as her own—a circumstance which caused her enemies to accuse her of a fondness for intrigue.

Miss Elphinstone's independence of character, joined to considerable personal attraction and a fortune of her own, had procured for her a number of admirers. Her correspondence and other available documents reveal the fact that she received formal proposals from the Duke of Clarence, afterwards William IV., when, in 1811 he was endeavouring to shake off Mrs. Jordan and her ten children; from Lord Dundonald, better known as Lord Cochrane, the inventor of the famous "secret war plan"—which has never yet been divulged; from Count Bothmer, of the King's German Legion, a soldier of fortune from Mecklenburg-Schwerin; from the Comte de

Balmain, the Russian who represented his government on the island of St. Helena during Napoleon's captivity; and from various other suitors of less notability. Amongst the aspirants to her hand were, it was said, the sixth Duke of Devonshire, who by dying a bachelor disappointed so many expectations, and Lord Byron, whose letters certainly contain some tender passages, and who presented her with an oriental costume which still figures amongst the family heirlooms. But no wife could have devoted herself more loyally than she did to her husband, and there can be little doubt that during the fifty years of their married life Flahault owed much to her exertions on his behalf, both in the social and political world. She died in 1867, four years before her husband.

It has already been stated that the Flahaults had a family of five daughters. Of these, two did not outlive their childhood, another (Louise) became a chronic invalid and died very soon after the close of this correspondence, while a fourth (Georgine) married some years later Félix, Marquis de Lavalette, sometime French Ambassador and Minister of the Interior. Only the eldest daughter, Emily, was, at the period with which we are dealing, married; curiously enough

INTRODUCTION

her husband, Lord Shelburne, was the grandson
of the Lord Lansdowne who had so warmly
befriended her own grandmother (Madame de
Souza) in England during her enforced emigration
nearly sixty years before. Lord Shelburne was
a Liberal Member of Parliament, and his father,
the third Marquis of Lansdowne, sometimes
called the "Nestor of the Whigs," was now
President of the Council in Lord John Russell's
ministry. Lady Shelburne thus found herself
surrounded by influences the reverse of friendly
to Louis Napoleon, while her mother, who (as
may be seen from the allusions to her visits to
Claremont and Esher) was still in close personal
relations with the Orleans family, was probably
little inclined at the outset to take a favourable
view of the President's doings.

As we have seen, it was under Talleyrand
that Flahault graduated in the school of European
diplomacy. From some unpublished letters of
that statesman I have extracted a sentence on
Anglo-French relations which, though written
nearly a hundred years ago, is so curiously applicable to-day, that I have used it in the place of
a dedication for this volume. Flahault, from his
connections in this country, must have already
been strongly predisposed towards it; it is none

the less interesting to see that his inclinations were thus reinforced by so potent a mentor.

After the Revolution of 1848, he appears to have made up his mind that the best chance of salvation for his own country lay in its return to some form of monarchical government. When Louis Napoleon appeared upon the scene, Flahault was naturally drawn towards him, both by recollections of his uncle and by the tie which had bound him to the Prince's mother. Thenceforward, while working for the advancement of the President's position in France, he lost no opportunity of enlisting, so far as he was able, the sympathies of the British Government.

He was peculiarly fitted for such an office, for, while he held no official position in either country, he had in both many highly placed friends. We shall see that he could not accomplish much with the Prince Consort, and still less with Queen Victoria; but he had the ear of the Prime Minister, Lord John Russell, as well as that of several of his colleagues in the Government. Public opinion in England, more especially in the ruling circle of the Whigs, was seriously upset by the events of December, 1851, and it was probably due in no small degree to Flahault's influence that, after the first marks of disapproval, the *coup d'état* was accepted with a tolerably good grace on this side of the Channel.

We have stated that Flahault's support of Louis Napoleon did not meet with unmixed approval in his home circle. For this reason perhaps, little was said about it in after years amongst his relatives. The not unimportant part played by him in all these events has thus remained practically unknown to his descendants and still more so to the outside public.

The career of Auguste de Morny is sufficiently well known, but a few details as to his early years, culled from the Flahault archives, may perhaps be usefully added to an account of events in which he occupies so prominent a place. The closest secrecy had been preserved as to his parentage. An obscure couple—by name Jean Hyacinthe de Morny and Emilie Coralie his wife—who appear to have been under some kind of obligation to M. de Souza, were produced at the critical moment of his birth, and duly claimed the child as their own. Both these supposititious parents disappeared—rather conveniently—a few years afterwards, but not before Jean de Morny had made his last will and testament. By this instrument, which is amongst the Flahault papers, he left all

his worldly goods—possibly also supposititious—
to the child, and appointed as the infant's
guardians the Souzas, whom failing, this responsibility was to fall on Charles de Flahault.
One cannot but applaud the ingenuity of an
arrangement which, while shielding the parents
from the consequences of their indiscretion, gave
to the real father the legal control of the child!
The plan, it must be admitted, worked admirably.
Auguste was soon put out to nurse, though he was
always within reach of his devoted grandmother,
who kept his father constantly informed of his
welfare. But in 1816, when both Flahault and
Hortense had left France, Madame de Souza insisted in gratifying her long-cherished desire to
have the boy under her own roof, and thenceforward Auguste became a member of the Souza
household. If his grandmother's letters are to be
believed, he must have been an attractive as well
as a precocious child—all his sayings and doings
are faithfully recorded by his fond relative and
by her Portuguese husband, who seems to have
been strangely captivated by the charm of his
wife's unacknowledged grandson.

After a time Flahault began once more to pay
occasional visits to Paris, sometimes accompanied
by his wife and children, and Auguste then made

the acquaintance of his "step-mother" and half-sisters; thenceforward he became a recognised member of the family, and soon we find him staying with them in England. In 1829, Morny was taken on a round of visits to some of Flahault's friends, where he acquitted himself with some credit on the occasion of his first introduction to a Scotch grouse moor. We hear of him again in one of the last of Mme. de Souza's letters which are extant, at the moment when the Revolution of July, 1830, broke out. Auguste was then 19 years of age, and his grandmother informs his father that he is off to join in the fray. The smell of powder, she says, has gone to his head, and nothing will stop him from enrolling in the *Garde nationale.* But no harm befell him, and not long afterwards he entered the legitimate profession of arms under King Louis Philippe.

His activities between 1830 and 1848 as soldier, financier, and leader of society, have been described by his biographer, M. Frédéric Loliée, and need not here be recapitulated.

During his later years the Duc de Morny employed for a time as confidential secretary the future novelist, Alphonse Daudet. Daudet afterwards made use of the information he had thus gained to portray his former master as the *Duc de Mora* in the novel *Le Nabab*. The portrait, in so far as it professes to describe Morny's *aventures galantes*, is certainly unkind and probably exaggerated; it is true nevertheless that he was extremely susceptible to the gentler sex.

Some ten years before the present correspondence opens, he had first met the Comtesse le Hon. She was the wife of the Belgian Ambassador in Paris, was famed for her beauty, and had inherited from her father, a banker named Mosselmann, an ample fortune. Morny and she soon became not only the closest of friends, but also partners in many business speculations. They lived next to each other in the Champs Élysées, Morny's house being, as we are told in contemporary memoirs, known as "La Loge à Fidèle." Flahault's house was not far off, and hence Madame le Hon will generally be found alluded to in his letters from Paris as "the neighbour." It is easy to see between the lines of his correspondence that, though circumstances often brought them together, he had a somewhat lively mistrust of the lady's opinions and of her influence on Auguste.

The liaison continued until 1857. In that

year Morny, while on a mission to St. Petersburg, married the Russian Princess Sophie Troubetskoi, and his partnership with the "Ambassadress of the golden hair" had perforce to come to an end. But the marriage wounded Madame le Hon in her tenderest susceptibilities and she made no secret of the fact. Some painful recriminations ensued, financial as well as personal, and the Emperor himself was in the end forced to intervene in order to preserve the peace and effect a settlement.

In the foregoing pages I have given an account which may serve to introduce the principal correspondents in the pages which follow. For the rest I must refer my readers to the short biographical notes which will be found in the Index at the end of the volume.

It remains only to say a word about the correspondence itself. As already mentioned, this is principally drawn from the Flahault family papers. During the course of a long married life Madame de Flahault kept almost every letter which her husband wrote to her. It will be observed that these were, at the period with which we are concerned, in English, though his earlier letters to her were written in French. Madame de Flahault spoke and wrote her husband's language fluently, but she seems nevertheless to have liked to be addressed in her own tongue. To his daughters, however, Flahault continued always to write in French. The English letters have been printed without alteration, omitting only such portions as appeared to be of no interest. The rest, including all letters to and from Louis Napoleon and Morny, have been translated from the French, and are distinguished by an asterisk.

A few documents have been added to the collection from the unpublished papers of my great-grandfather Henry, third Marquis of Lansdowne. These relate to the dismissal of Palmerston in December, 1851; their inclusion seemed to be indicated both by their general relevance to the subject-matter in hand, and by the close relations which existed between Palmerston and Flahault.

Few of the original letters are dated, many bear only the day of the week on which they were written, and some do not even give that information. It has therefore, for the most part, been necessary to place the documents by means of their allusions to passing events.

The correspondence, as will at once be seen, is by no means consecutive. There are consider-

INTRODUCTION

able periods when, Flahault being at home, no written communications passed between him and his wife. If Morny's letters had all been kept, they would have filled these gaps with material which could scarcely have failed to be interesting, but unfortunately with the exception of those written in the year 1852, very few are still extant.

I have endeavoured to give to the narrative some sort of continuity by prefacing a note to each of the three sections into which the book is divided, and where particular letters seem to require it, by similarly prefixing to them a few words of explanation.

KERRY.

Bowood,
January, 1924.

I

BEFORE THE COUP D'ÉTAT

(1848–1851)

I

THE Revolution of February, 1848, which drove King Louis Philippe into exile at Claremont, deprived at the same time the Comte de Flahault of his post as French Ambassador in Vienna. He lost no time in rejoining his wife and family in England, and his letters show that it was not till October in the following year that he revisited his own country.

Morny meanwhile remained in France, whence he no doubt kept Flahault fully informed of all that was passing, while from time to time he crossed the Channel for a short stay with his relatives in England.

The letter with which the correspondence opens —the only surviving one from Morny of this period —was written a few weeks before the Presidential Election of December 10, 1848. It reports a conversation which had just taken place between Dr. Véron, the editor of the *Constitutionnel*, and

General Cavaignac, who, since the suppression of the popular risings in June, had virtually occupied the position of Dictator, and was at the time the official republican candidate for the Presidency. Another account of the same meeting has been given by Véron himself in his *Mémoires d'un Bourgeois de Paris*, published in 1855. It may perhaps be taken as a testimony to the veracity of both narrators that the two versions do not differ in any important particular. It was a conversation which probably had far-reaching consequences, for, as Morny explains, it brought about the definite adhesion, not only of the *Constitutionnel*, but of Thiers, to the cause of Louis Napoleon, and thus assured him a triumphant majority in the election. Although Thiers was afterwards to change his mind, Véron remained faithful to the Prince-President, and the *Constitutionnel* was instrumental in obtaining popular approval for his subsequent policy, including the *coup d'état* two years later.

Amongst his many financial activities Morny had some years earlier bought a large share in the *Constitutionnel;* this had thrown him into close relations with its editor, and it is not unlikely that it was this connection which first brought him into personal contact with the President.

BEFORE THE COUP D'ÉTAT

Morny to Flahault

PARIS, *November* 1848.

My dear friend,[1]

Paris has been much excited over a conversation, said to have taken place between Cavaignac and Véron, and—with the help of some words that fell from Thiers and other politicians—I have now discovered the whole story. The facts, which I have obtained from Véron himself, are as follows. They are sufficiently curious to justify my reporting them to you.

To understand the position of the speakers, you must go back two or three months, when there arose amongst those who are about General Cavaignac the question of the suppression of the *Constitutionnel* newspaper. This was politically speaking a serious undertaking, for the *Constitutionnel*, which had always supported moderation and order, had behind it some politicians of repute, and though the calculated opposition of the paper had annoyed him, the "Dictator" hesitated to take action against it.

There came one day a Representative, who happened to be at once a friend of Cavaignac's

---

[1] *Mon cher ami*—Flahault and Morny always addressed each other thus, and they preferred the employment of the pronoun *vous* to the more familiar *tu*.

and a former colleague of Véron's, to see the latter, and asked him if it would be disagreeable to him to visit the General. "If he asks for me," said Véron, "I have no reason for not going to him. I would indeed do so with pleasure, but at the same time I have no reason for going uninvited." The next day the mutual friend came to fetch him and took him to the General. The General received him politely and, having invited him to sit down said, "Why is it that you dislike me? Have I not rendered good services both to Society and to your own party?" To this Véron replied in effect, "I do not dislike you. My paper voices the opinion of moderate people, and its party, which is far from being dead, is not that to which you belong. All the same I do not dislike you. I have nothing to regret, for I had no personal relations with those who have gone under. As to the King and the Princes, I have had more reason to find fault with them than otherwise. Hence I have no feeling or interest of a personal kind in the matter. You can therefore rely on my policy being loyal. If you will give us an honest and a moderate Republic, we will not only not work against you, but we will support you." After the exchange of a few more words in this sense, Véron as he

THE HON. MARGARET MERCER ELPHINSTONE

(From a miniature by G. L. Saunders, 1812)

was leaving received an invitation to come again. To this he replied, "General, I am not in a position to come and see you informally, but whenever you want to talk politics with me, send me a message. I will come with pleasure, and if you want any news inserted or confirmed in my paper, you have only to let me know; I shall always be delighted to make myself personally useful to you."

I had forgotten to say that during the course of this conversation, while he was speaking of the political future, the General had said, "At any rate I am certain of 600 votes in the Chamber in favour of the nomination of the President by the Assembly." Since this vote, which destroyed the hopes of Cavaignac and his party, was given, the General has suffered from constant irritability, his conversation has become abrupt, his talk full of veiled threats. Véron heard no more of him.

A few days ago the mutual friend returned, and suggested to Véron that he might again pay a visit to Cavaignac, a proposal which the former refused, on the plea that he would only go when asked. The next day Véron received under cover a pass to admit him to the President of the Council. He made no move. Last Friday at eight o'clock in the morning, there comes a man to Véron's house, who without giving his name insists on seeing him. Véron, who never gets up before noon and is inaccessible before that hour, refused to see him, more especially since he did not know who his visitor might be. In the end this person said: "You may say it is an Aide-de-Camp of General Cavaignac and that the General is anxious to see M. Véron this morning." To this Véron replied that he was free only from three o'clock until midnight. At 5 o'clock the Aide-de-Camp reappeared and made an appointment for 11 o'clock. At 11 o'clock Véron was with the General. Cavaignac was seated at his writing-table; he seemed to be angry, his brow was clouded. In a dry tone he thus began:

"M. Véron, I have asked you to come and see me in order that I might explain myself quite frankly; allow me therefore with soldierly frankness to go straight to the point and to put you this question: In the matter of the Presidency, are you for me or against me?"

"Your question, General, is a somewhat blunt and peremptory one. 'For you' and 'against you.' In such cases it is a question of degree."[1]

"There may be degrees, but I don't like degrees,

[1] *Il y a des nuances.*

and it is precisely for that reason that I ask you if you are for me or against me."

These words, spoken in a dry and haughty tone, rather wounded Véron's feelings. He rose and said:

"Upon my word, M. le Président, since you talk of frankness, I will take you at your word. Pray tell me why is it that you expect us to show you so much sympathy? Have you not made this advance towards us both unwillingly and grudgingly? Are not your sympathies with the extremists well known and clear to all observers? Is it not a fact that you are in complete agreement with General La Moricière as regards the Law of Succession, a law which offends both the wishes and the feelings of the people of this country? You unwillingly appointed MM. Dufaure and Vivien; did you not then install in revenge M. Recurt for the Seine, M. Trouvé Chauvel in the Ministry of Finance and M. Gervais de Caen as Chief of Police?"[1]

"Ah, that's how it is," interrupted Cavaignac roughly; "you wish to have everything, you have no gratitude. Your party always behaves

[1] The first two Ministers held moderate views, but the last three, appointed by Cavaignac in October, 1848, had pronounced leanings towards the Socialist party.

like this, you are intractable; you are all the same—you have learnt nothing and forgotten nothing."

"But, General, our party, which you treat so lightly, is that of the majority in the country—yours is that of the minority."

"Do you mean to say that it was a minority which brought about the Revolution in February and which caused the Republic to be generally accepted?"

"Well, General, people may say what they like about the Revolution of February, but I witnessed it. I was on the spot, you were not. It was nothing but a *coup de main* which happened to succeed."

"You call it a *coup de main*, well, so let it be —a *coup de main;* but the *coup de main* made the Republic, and the Republic will last. I will answer for that with my life; and taking it all in all, is our Republic so bad a thing? Is it distasteful to this country? Cannot one even now dine well, put on one's kid gloves[1] and hear good music?"

"Do tell me where one can hear good music, M. le Président." This little joke, which was intended to show how the Republic had ruined

[1] *Mettre des gants jaunes.*

everything, made the General still more angry. He made believe not to understand, and rose.

"Anyhow make no mistake, the Republic will last, I stake my reputation on it. You may say that it is the work of a minority, very well, but that minority will defend it to the last drop of its blood and by every means in their power. The misfortune is that you have two or three big newspapers with 90,000 regular subscribers apiece. Well, by God, we will take your subscribers from you, there will be no difficulty about that—mark my words, you had better consider your position."

"M. le Président, I have considered the matter fully, but permit me to say that your language is scarcely such as to make me decide in your favour the question which you put to me so emphatically at the outset of our conversation."

"Very well, sir."

"Very well, M. le Président."

"Good-bye, sir, and if you should wish to make any further communication to me, you know where to find me; if you come in the morning you can come in by the Rue de Varennes; if in the evening, by the other street."

"General, I shall neither come in the morning nor in the evening, unless, as I have already said, you do me the honour to ask for an interview.

I ask nothing and expect no favours from any one." So saying Véron bowed and withdrew, while the General with an injured and scornful air merely nodded and turned away, humming a tune.

Véron went off hot-foot to relate this conversation to Thiers. In their view, which was corroborated by certain indiscreet remarks of Cavaignac's associates, he was working for a *coup d'état*. They came to the conclusion that his inclinations were revolutionary, that he sympathises with the Flocons,[1] and that if he ever leant towards the moderates he did so unwillingly. Moreover they think him a bad character. It was Bugeaud who compared him to a cow in the skin of a hyaena.

So from that moment, with a view to getting rid of Cavaignac, Thiers and his party have worked for Prince Louis's election instead of for Cavaignac. It was they who resolved on the article on the Presidency which appeared in the *Constitutionnel* the day before yesterday, and this has still further annoyed Cavaignac's supporters in the Chamber.

Thiers to Flahault

The following note was evidently written in answer to a letter of condolence on the death of

[1] *I.e.* with the extreme revolutionaries—one of whom was so called.

some near relative of Thiers—probably his father-in-law, a banker named Dosne, who died about this time. It shows that Flahault, who in past years had been constantly thrown into relations with Thiers, was for the moment still on good terms with him. They were, however, soon to quarrel.

PARIS, *April* 16, 1849.

My dear Flahault,

I thank you for your kind marks of sympathy and assure you that I greatly appreciate them. We have lost a good man, a man who was at the same time wise, able and honest. He had worked all his life to assure a fortune for his children, and he saw part of his work destroyed by the odious revolution of 1848. The anxieties of this year had left him without the strength to fight an attack of cholera. He has left us a competence, which, if modest, is enough to allow us to live in independence; so we find ourselves poor but free. This is what we like, and were it not for our personal grief, we should in other respects be perfectly happy.

What a year it has been, and what a year the next will be! Let us at any rate keep the peace, —so that we may still be able to meet, and

honourable men of all countries may continue to
work together.

Good-bye. Please pay my respects to Mme.
de Flahault.—Ever yours,

A. THIERS.

Flahault to Morny

Napoleon Jérôme, better known in after years as
"Plon-Plon," from the distaste which he is said to
have evinced for the leaden bullets of the Crimea,
was the son of Jérôme Bonaparte, and therefore
first cousin to Louis Napoleon. He had from
the first been a thorn in the Prince's side, and
posed as the champion of the extreme revolutionaries, who—with recollections of their prototypes
of 1789—delighted to call themselves "La
Montagne."

To those who supported the Élysée, they became
known as the "Coquins"; and ingenious persons
invented a riddle: "Quel est la différence entre Napoleon et un chapon?" the answer to which may be
found in a play upon the words, "un Coquin
puissant."

In April, 1849, a scene took place between *Plon-
Plon* and the President. It was said that they
had nearly come to blows, and that they would
have done so had it not been for the forcible inter-

vention of Morny, assisted by *Plon-Plon's* sister, the Princess Mathilde. Not long before this *Plon-Plon* had been appointed Ambassador at Madrid, but on his way to that capital he made a speech so hostile to the President that the latter at once recalled him. He had just returned to Paris when this quarrel was reported to have taken place, and though it was afterwards officially contradicted in the *Moniteur*, it seems probable that it must have had a foundation in fact. The *Times* and *Morning Post* both mention the affair, but are silent as to the "coarse words" to which Flahault took such exception. It is clear, however, by the context that these must have had reference to the President's birth.

This matter has since been often discussed, and it is interesting to find that Flahault warmly repudiated the doubts which *Plon-Plon* had cast on the Prince's legitimacy. Louis Napoleon was born on April 20, 1808, and Flahault (as he himself now tells us) was, during the whole of the preceding year, on garrison duty in East Prussia; this disposes of a theory which has been sometimes advanced by those who did not know the facts, that Flahault himself was the father. It is clear, nevertheless, from his early letters, that he had been on friendly terms with Queen Hortense some time before 1808, and in view of the still closer relations which subsequently existed, Flahault may reasonably be expected to have known the true facts concerning Louis Napoleon's parentage.

Not less worthy of remark is Flahault's further assertion that the Emperor Napoleon I. was the son of the Comte de Marbeuf—the French military Governor of Corsica in the year 1769. It is well known that Marbeuf showed attentions to the handsome Mme. Laetitia Bonaparte, and that it was through his agency that her son Napoleon secured the advantages of a French education. Though rumour has generally stopped there, Flahault's testimony cannot be lightly dismissed. It is true that he was himself not born at the time, but his mother, as her letters show, was, during the early years of the First Empire, on the most confidential terms with Josephine. There can be little doubt that the view here expressed was that of the Empress and her immediate entourage.

The concluding paragraph of this letter supplies the year in which it was written, for the debate there alluded to must be that which took place in the House of Lords on Monday, May 7, 1849, on the Repeal of the Navigation Laws. This was the principal measure of Lord John Russell's Government during that session, and it was in the end carried, though by a small majority.

L[ONDON], May 4 [1849].

Is the newspaper report of a scene between P[rince] L[ouis] and his cousin a true story? What a *coquin* the latter seems to be! Good God, is experience to teach them nothing and must the same mistakes always be made by this wretched family? How the Emperor[1] suffered at their hands! I am sure that nothing could be more certain than that Napoleon's[2] coarse words were false. We were at the time in Prussia, but I have heard it said that the King and Queen were brought together as a consequence of the misfortune which they had suffered in the loss of their eldest son. In all this the hatred of the Bonapartes for the Beauharnais comes out once again, as it did in times past. Every one here is furious with Napoleon.

Good-bye—send me a line. Prince Louis should be very careful about his diplomatic appointments even in the minor posts. Believe me this is most important, especially at the Courts where rival claimants to the throne are to be found. I do not know of any more infamous action than

---

[1] Napoleon I. [2] Plon-Plon.

that of joining a Government for the express purpose of betraying it, but such things are done all the same.

As a young man I always heard it said that the Emperor was the son of M. de Marbeuf. Good-bye, my dear friend, I embrace you with all my heart.

Monday's debate will last two days, but there is increasing confidence that the Government will carry the day.

Morny to Madame de Flahault

The *Assemblée Constituante*, which had hitherto formed the legislature of the Republic, was now, by the terms of the constitution, to be replaced by a new chamber—the *Assemblée Législative*. The letter which follows was written just after the elections (May 13) and before the declaration of the poll. Its principal interest lies in Morny's account of his relations with the President at this period. It seems to have been generally assumed that Morny did not become intimate with Louis Napoleon till much later, and M. Loliée, Morny's biographer, actually states (p. 91) that their first interview took place *after* the elections of 1849. It now becomes clear that this must be revised and that Morny had by then been for some time in the

Prince's confidence. It will be observed that Morny even then was thinking of "Empire" as a solution of his country's troubles.

His pessimistic forecasts as to the election were not realised. He himself was duly elected for the department of Puy de Dôme in Auvergne, and only 180 Socialists in all were returned in the new assembly of 700 members. If contemporary accounts are to be believed, Morny, in spite of his position at the Élysée, stood as an Orleanist and was elected by the help of the Royalist committee of the Rue de Poitiers.

[PARIS] *May* 16 [1849].

Dear Madame de Flahault,

You are very good to think so much of my health and to offer me such a pleasant refuge from the cholera.[1] I should, I can assure you, be delighted to take advantage of it, even if there was no cholera, but there is a political "cholera" coming which, as it seems to me, may become even more serious than anything which we have yet experienced; and I cannot go away, more especially in view of the position which I have taken up and of the trust which the Prince

[1] There was a bad outbreak of cholera in Paris in the spring and summer of 1849.

95

places in me. I see him once at least, and often
twice a day. He discusses everything with me
both persons and events. Could I desert him
with decency at such a critical moment? It is
really impossible.

It seems that the elections will not be as good
as was expected. Socialism has made the most
alarming strides; in several of the Departments
the Red candidates will be successful, and even
if the Moderates succeed in others, their majority,
will be so small that the moral effect will be
disastrous. If this happens there will be nothing
left to do but to pack our things, get up a civil
war and ask the Cossacks to come and help us!
I smile in writing thus, and I expect your national
pride will be up in arms against me, but I give
you my word, if you were to come into contact with socialists you would infinitely prefer
the Cossacks. There must be limits to one's
patriotism!

It is difficult to tell you everything, but you
may take my word for it that, if the Chamber
turns out badly, we are done for in a week;
if it is less bad, we may last a month. The
Empire is the only thing that can save the
situation. Some of the principal politicians
have been nibbling at the idea, but the Prince

has conscientious scruples. Anyhow within a short time great events will be certain to take place.

I think I shall be returned in Auvergne, but they tell me that the Reds will secure many votes, and if they do I shall be defeated. I shall regret it—no more than that! for God only knows what will be the fate of this new Assembly. Thank you once more, dear Madame de Flahault, and believe me, Your most sincerely devoted

AUGUSTE.

M. de Flahault would be wrong to come at this moment. He could do no good. He is connected with no party and would commit himself to no purpose.

Duchess of Orleans to Madame de Flahault

Flahault had been principal equerry to King Louis Philippe's eldest son, the Duke of Orleans, who was killed in a carriage accident in 1842. The Duke left a widow—née Princess Helène of Mecklenburg-Schwerin—with whom the female members of the Flahault family still kept up close relations. The Duchess's son, the Comte de Paris, was now, of course, the direct Orleanist heir to the French throne, but being still an infant he could scarcely be considered as an effective competitor against Louis Napoleon as *de facto* ruler. Many of the Orleanists justified their support of the Prince-President on the score that it might make the restoration of the younger branch possible in the future.

When the French royal family took up their quarters at Claremont, the Duchess with her infant son established herself at Esher close by. The Château d'Eisenach from which she now writes was in Gotha; it had been placed at her disposal for the time being by her uncle, the Duke of Saxe-Weimar.

EISENACH, 23 *September* 1849.

I had meant, my dear Madame de Flahault, to write and bid you goodbye before I left England; to tell you how glad I had been to see you again, and to find you ever the same, full of understanding and of affection, but I did not have the time. It was all taken up by family duties, and I was forced to defer the pleasure until my return to Germany. Even here I have found a thousand duties which had to be performed, a thousand family affairs to be attended to, a thousand visits from my friends which claimed my time as hostess; but still I feel that I can delay no longer, in thought at any rate, from grasping your hand. I trust that this letter will be luckier than my first one was, and that it will reach you, so that you may receive these assurances of my affectionate regard and of my tender sympathy. I hope it may at the same time serve to recall me to Emilie,[1] whom I was so pleased to see once more, and that when I come again to England, she will give me rather more of her time, so that we may compare notes of those bygone days, which were precious to her as they were to me, and to which I am always glad to return in thought. Please thank her also for her delightful but all too short visit, and remember me to Monsieur de Flahault, whom I will invite next spring. . . .

I found Germany in a peaceful state and enjoying the repose she has so dearly bought. She is not at the moment occupied by questions of democracy; she is more taken up just now by the ideals of nationalism, and political developments in Prussia, Austria, Bavaria, and Saxony. Since neither the principle of monarchy nor the foundations of society are here involved, one can regard these questions without much anxiety. We have not reached this point in our unhappy

[1] Madame de Flahault's eldest daughter, Lady Shelburne.

France, and there are still many questions which must be solved before we can enjoy the peace which is our neighbours'. One can only hope that our country will learn something from the sharp lessons she has received.

My mother asks me to give you a thousand affectionate messages, and my children also desire that I should remember them kindly to you. Think of me sometimes, my dear Madame de Flahault, and remember that your true friendship has been bestowed on one whose heart is not ungrateful. With kindest remembrances,

HELÈNE.

Flahault to Madame de Flahault

Morny was now in England, and the objections which he had raised to Flahault's proposed visit to Paris earlier in the year must have been overcome. They went there together in October, and a meeting with the Prince-President was arranged forthwith. In 1831, Talleyrand had written from London to the Ambassador-designate for Berlin: "Je ne sais pas si l'on vous aura écrit que la duchesse de St. Leu est ici avec son jeune fils . . . Cela vous ferait-il prendre votre route par ici pour aller à Berlin? J'en serais charmé. Londres, Hambourg, Berlin—cela n'allonge guère." It would seem, however, that this opportunity of a family reunion was allowed to slip, and that Flahault had in fact never seen the future Emperor since the days of his childhood.

The extracts which follow are all taken from letters addressed (as always, in English) by Flahault to his wife.

RICHMOND, *Sunday* [*Sept.* 30, 1849].

My dear Margaret,

. . . I am just returned from visiting Mme. de Lieven with Auguste. Poor woman, how bored she must be, if one judges by the joy she feels when one enters her room! It appears from the letters she had received from Warsaw, that the report of the bad reception of General Lamoricière[1] sent to the English Government by the English Consul is not true, or at least very much exaggerated. But what is funny is to see this friend of Cavaignac and representative of the Republick, flatter the Emperor as much as he can. At one of the Reviews he said to him—"Il est facile d'avoir un bon système politique, quand il est appuyé par de belles troupes." He was invited with the rest of the Corps Diploma-

---

[1] General La Moricière was sent as Ambassador Extraordinary to Nicholas I., Emperor of Russia, in the autumn of 1849.

tique to the ceremony of the procession of the *drapeaux* taken from the Hungarians, and had to kneel down with all the rest for thanksgiving for the Russian victories. However when they rose the Emperor said to him: "Général, vous avez cueilli dans les rues de Paris au mois de juin les premiers lauriers de la gloire que nous célébrons." Well said, don't you think?

What a rascally set are all that Dufaure Toqueville and Beaumont party, holding up high republican principles in publick, and privately abusing the republick and hunting after all the places.

Princess Metternich has just been here. They have not been able to procure a house at Brussels, and are going to send Richard there with Mme. Artaud. I don't place much reliance on Richard's *savoir faire*, but suppose Mme. Artaud will supply what he wants. . . .

RICHMOND, *Oct. 3* [1849].

. . . I should like you to be in London before I go to Paris. I have received a letter from M. de Chabannes informing me of the Duchess of Orleans having sent him a letter for you,[1] which she desires him to transmit safely, and asking if he was to send it to me or begging to have your

[1] Her letter of September 23.

direction. I have just answered him and desired him to direct it to Tullyallan.

What do you say of the Constantinople news?[1] Is it possible that the peace of the world, that has not been broken by the Revolution of 1830 of Belgium, of Poland, and all those of 1848, should be destroyed for the sake of a set of revolutionary scoundrels? It would be too bad—and yet I don't see how it can be avoided. The Emperor Nicholas having once made the demand of extradition, cannot recede without abandoning the policy constantly followed by Russia at Constantinople—that of the master over the vassal; and on the other hand the Sultan, (being young), and Rechid Pasha, (having imbibed in France and England civilized notions), are not likely to give way, being backed by what the papers call the magnanimous and gallant—but what I should call the wrong headed—Canning, and foolish Aupick: for I think their business was to try to smooth down matters instead of fanning the flame.

What is then to happen?—A general war,

[1] The Austrian revolutionary movement having been defeated, Kossuth, Bem, and other leaders took refuge in Turkey. The Emperor Nicholas of Russia then joined with the Austrian Government in demanding their extradition, which the Sultan refused, but only when he was assured of British support in doing so.

bloodshed and universal ruin of Kossuth and Bem. I hope however that the Austrian Government which has no wish to go to Constantinople or interest in the destruction of the Ottoman Empire, will confine its action to a suspension of diplomatic relations, and let Russia (who wants no assistance) settle her own quarrel with the Porte. This will deprive P.[1] of the opportunity of recommencing his operations in Italy. A propos have you read a note of Temple's to the Neapolitan Government, published in the *Chronicle*, with the most charming reply of the Minister Fortunato?—fortunate indeed to have it in his power to write such a reply. But how can an English minister expose himself to such just and humiliating rebuffs! Poor Mme. de Lieven is in despair at the notion of having to leave France and England,[2] I daresay she has the boldness to blame her Emperor's imprudence *au fond de son cœur*. Adieu, my dearest Margaret, I embrace you with all my heart.

[LONDON] *Tuesday* 9 [*October* 1849].

I am just returned from Mivarts where I have bid adieu to the poor old Prince,[3] whom I daresay

[1] Palmerston.
[2] Because her husband, Prince de Lieven, was a Russian diplomat.
[3] Metternich.

BEFORE THE COUP D'ÉTAT

I shall never see again, though I promised him
to go and pay him a visit either at Brussels or
Johannisberg next year. He desired me to say
a thousand things to you and Georgy,[1] and that
he was sorry not to have shaken hands with you
both. Mme. Sandor, Hermione and Mélanie[2]
stay here till Thursday.

I dined yesterday at old Lady Grey's with
Sir George Grey, Charles Wood, Lord Carlisle
and Lady Tankerville, it was very agreeable.
The conversation was not very political, but from
the little that was said I am in hope that the
Constantinople storm will blow over. Fourteen
of the refugees with Bem at their head have
embraced the Mahomedan religion—Zamoyski is
not one of them.

I do not know what tune you allude to that
you were singing to which we would not listen,
but if you mean that in the assistance given to
Austria by the Emperor Nicholas, there were any
views of private ambition to be gratified, you
are the only one in Europe who pretends such a
thing. His demand of the extradition of these
men has only for its object that guilt should not
remain unpunished, and really it is high time that

[1] Flahault's second daughter, afterwards Marquise de Lavalette.
[2] Metternich's daughters.

justice should have its course. I am not at all flattered by your assimilation of me with these circulating conspirators. I have never been concerned in any conspiracy, and in 1815 only joined Napoleon when Louis XVIII. had left Paris; and I cannot accept your *rapprochement*. If anything was to result out of this squabble and one drop of blood was split it would be more than the heads of all those refugees are worth. . . .

Adieu, I hope you are not going to remain too long with your gardeners.[1] There have been 114 cases of cholera at Alnwick, so pray don't come that way.

[LONDON] *Saturday* [*Oct.* 13, 1849].

I want to talk with you before I go to Paris and I should prefer going with Auguste to going alone. . . .

PARIS, *Saturday* [*27 October* 1849].

I have just got your letter of yesterday and thank you for this early proof of your souvenir.

My first letter will have proved to you that while the wind was howling at 12 o'clock, we were tossed about and I was as sick as a poor dog. . . . I dined yesterday at Passy with *all*

---

[1] At Tullyallan, in Scotland, where Mme. de Flahault was laying out a large garden at the time.

106

the family, Auguste and Carbonel. Villa Real was asked to meet me but was pre-engaged. Today I dine with my neighbour,[1] but before that I am to pay a visit to the P. I do not know if his star is on the decline, but depend on it that Lady T.'s[2] candidate has no chance.

I called yesterday upon poor Mme. d'Audenarde, and only think of my horror, when the servant told me she had been ill for 3 months and was *à toute extrémité*. I saw d'Audenarde who confirmed the sad report. I have seen Mme. de Lieven, who appears enchanted to be again in her entresol.

Adieu, my dear Margaret. Give this letter to the children and embrace them for me. I embrace you with all my heart.

[PARIS] *Monday* [*Oct.* 29, 1849].

I wrote yesterday to Georgina that my visit to the P. had been put off on account of a bad ache (*sic*) to which it appears he is very subject. I am to see him this morning, and I wish the visit was over.

Yesterday I paid many visits, but found

[1] Mme. le Hon.
[2] Lady Tankerville is no doubt intended, and her candidate was the Prince de Joinville, who was being talked of as a possible successor to Louis Napoleon when the latter's term of office came to an end in 1852.

107

nobody. At Molé's the porter, a sort of *bonne femme* with a round cap said he was not at home; but I suppose her conscience smiting her (very extraordinary considering whose door she keeps!) she asked me if I was a *Représentant;* "Because" said she, "he is at home, but I have orders to admit only a few *Représentants"*—I left my card and went away.

I dined at the ——[1] with the most extraordinary party you could imagine: 2 Ladies, Mme. Leroux, mother in law to Bauffremont's son, and Mme. Conrad Lagrange, a sort of Greek tragic muse, dressed like a mountebank. Luttrel Bauffremont, Richelieu, Bellocq and a Secretary of the Tuscan legation to whom she gave her arm to go to dinner, which was perfectly ridiculous. The first word she said to me was to beg that I would not mention A. W.[2] being here. As it is a secret (which I did not know) desire the girls not to mention it. I cannot bear knowing those things that are to be kept secret, and cannot conceive why *he* called upon me after

---

[1] Flahault has omitted the name of his hostess, but she was evidently Madame le Hon, "the neighbour."

[2] The initials are those of Count Alexandre Walewski, with whom the Flahault family were (see *infra*) intimate. It is not apparent, however, why it should have been so profound a secret that Walewski was in Paris.

never having done me that honour in London! Holland is going to London for change of air.

After dinner Auguste came to take me and we went to Thiers, who, after one has not seen him for some time, appears always (notwithstanding his *esprit*) more ill bred and *dépourvu* of tact. I don't know if the Republican régime has increased these defects, but his language and coarse expressions are intolerable. . . . Roger was at Thiers and enquired much for you.

I went yesterday all over our house and found it very clean and nice. The gilding is quite astonishing; the only thing necessary would be to paint or distemper the *salon d'angle*.

[PARIS] *Tuesday* [*Oct.* 30, 1849].

I paid my visit[1] yesterday. I must put off till we meet giving you the details of our conversation, but can only say that nothing could exceed the kindness of the reception I met with. When I entered he took me by the hand and said that I was mixed up with all his oldest recollections and hoped that he might consider me as an old friend. Our interview lasted over an hour and we talked much of the past and more of the present—but as I said, that must

[1] *I.e.* to the Prince Louis Napoleon.

be kept. . . . I meant to go Saturday but I must stay to dine with the P. I have seen the Princess Mathilde who has enquired *tenderly* for you—now I am going to Jérome.

[PARIS] *Thursday* [*Nov.* 1, 1849].

Yesterday was a sort of *crise* and there was a sort of alarm. I did not partake in it, because I had no doubt that however disagreeable the change might be to the chiefs of the majority,[1] the necessity for them and the majority itself to remain united to the President, is so great that their separation from him is impossible. It appears that he is determined to take every means both as to measures and men for the establishment of order. Yesterday Auguste saw him at the moment the change was taking place and he was as quiet as if nothing was doing.[2] It was evident to me when I saw him that his mind was made up to get out of his present position. It appears that although very quiet and gentle, nothing has any effect upon him when his determination is once taken. I dine

[1] The so-called *Burgraves*—Thiers, Molé, de Broglie, etc.
[2] On Wednesday, October 31, the President had by means of a brief message to the assembly dismissed the whole of Odilon Barrot's ministry and substituted another under the nominal leadership of General d'Hautpoul. This event marked the definite abandonment of government by the legislature.

with him on Monday and my intention is to set out on Tuesday. . . . I have ordered your grey gown with the approbation of Auguste & Co. and hope it will meet with yours.

*Guizot to Flahault

Guizot, who had for so long been foreign minister to King Louis Philippe, fled with that monarch at the outbreak of the Revolution, but returned to Paris the following year. Henceforth he worked for the so-called *fusion* of the claims of the elder and younger branch of the Bourbons in the person of the Comte de Chambord, though he never attempted to return to political life. Flahault had of course been in the closest relations with him in the past, but the following was apparently the only communication which passed between them during the Presidential period. Henry Greville found Guizot unsatisfactory as a conversationalist— "Il débite et ne cause pas." A similar criticism might be applied to this letter.

PARIS, 20 *December* 1849.

My dear Count,

I have promised to recommend to you, and I do so with the greatest pleasure, M. Gueneau de Mussy, who is the bearer of this letter. You are of course aware that he is the doctor whom M. Chomel sent to the King, and who took such care of them and did them so much good during their imprisonment. . . .

I cannot tell you anything about matters here, which you do not know or cannot guess. There are plenty of suggestions, but nobody has the determination to put them into effect. Every one gets as far as the edge of the ditch, but nobody will jump it. Matters will drag on like this for some time—probably until the general election comes near. Are not the dangers sufficiently evident and sufficiently grave, to give, to every one, a little foresight and courage? I cannot say! Meanwhile I think that we should get through the winter in peace.—Always yours, my dear Count, GUIZOT.

Flahault to Madame de Flahault

We now find Flahault once more in Paris, whence as before he communicates frequently—if briefly—with his wife. He was ostensibly occupied with arrangements concerning the pension to which he was entitled as a General on the retired list, and with the disposal of his house in Paris, but he found time between whiles to see a good deal of the President and of his friends. The Flahaults' house

was at the corner of the Rue d'Angoulême (afterwards the Rue de Morny and Rue de la Boétie) and
the Champs Élysées. They had bought it some
twenty years previously, but, having determined
that he would take no part in the affairs of the
Republic, Flahault now resolved to dispose of it.
It was let and eventually sold to Baroness Roger,
the widow of Regnier, Marquis de Massa. Close
to it, and also fronting on the Champs Élysées, was
the house of Madame le Hon, generally referred to
in this correspondence as "the neighbour." Next
door to her was Auguste de Morny, with whom
Flahault stayed when his own house was no
longer available.

The principal excitement in Paris during this
visit of Flahault's were the by-elections occasioned
by the unseating of 30 members of the Assembly
who had been concerned in an attempted Socialist
rising in the previous year.

In the event 10 of the seats were won from the
Socialist party, but for the 3 vacancies in Paris, the
"Reds" succeeded in again returning their nomi-
nees. This result was largely responsible for the
subsequent raising of the suffrage by the *Loi
électorale* of May, 1850.

Flahault returned to London about the middle of
March.

THE SECRET OF THE COUP D'ÉTAT

I am here after a rough passage. . . . I am going by the 3 o'clock train and hope to be in Paris at 11 o'clock.

PARIS, *Thursday, Feby.* 28 [1850].

B. has not brought my order of the Legion of Honor and I wish you to send it to me by the French Courier, who I believe leaves London tomorrow evening. . . . The plaque is the one with the effigy of Napoleon, and the chain with 4 little crosses is in a small *carton* tied up with some tape. . . . Don't neglect this for I should be embarrassed if I had to dine with the President.

If you have any news give them to me. There is a belief here that the English administration is threatened¹ and I have damaged many a joy, Pss. L[ieven] *en tête*, by expressing a contrary opinion.

Mrs. John Stanley is here for at least a fortnight longer and I am sorry to hear that Clifden has again fallen into Mme. d'Orties *filets*. I saw yesterday Lady Holland, who spoke to me

---

¹ There was a ministerial crisis in March, 1850.

114

long and to whom I answered with much sincerity
—but I leave that till we meet.

Your glass cabinet in the *salon vert* is 4 ft.
3½ inches high and 4 ft. 1½ inches wide.

[*Feb.* 1850.]

After much consideration Auguste has decided
not to sell his pictures this year and begs that
you will apprize Christie's of this determination.

[PARIS] *Monday* 4 [*March* 1850].

The house is let for 15,000 fr. till the 31st of
December and 18,000 fr. per annum, till the end
of the year 1852. . . .

I move to Auguste's tomorrow and as soon as
my pension is settled I will start.

I dine tomorrow at the Prince Louis' and am
this moment going to the Grand Duchess.[1] My
letter of yesterday was to be taken by Ld. Clifden,
but as he had put off his journey till today I sent
it by the post.

I told you Auguste does not sell his pictures;
you will therefore I suppose paint in distemper,
which can be renewed easily should the pictures
be sold next year, and at all events the silk could
be put on it.

[1] Stéphanie de Bade, the President's cousin.

THE SECRET OF THE COUP D'ÉTAT

Wednesday [March 6, 1850],
from Auguste's [PARIS].

I am just come from the Grand Duchess where I have breakfasted and seen the President. It is lucky that I am not staying here, for he exercises a sort of fascination over me which would be dangerous considering the line I wish to keep —and what is extraordinary is that it is from his simplicity and candid manner!

Your letter of the 4 reached me late last night and is very interesting. . . . I am much pressed to stay here a little longer.

[PARIS] *Saturday [March 9, 1850].*

I went this morning at 10 o'clock to see the P[resident], had a long talk with him and breakfasted there. Nothing can be better, kinder, more unaffected than he is. He asked me to see him again but I must be off.

Madame Roger is in the house and much dissatisfied with it. Toussaint sent me word that she wished to let it again.

Here is Delessert who desires me to say 1000 things to you. . . .

[PARIS] *Monday [March 11, 1850].*

Nothing so tiresome as being always in a hurry and that is my case here. I must now go immediately to the Grand Duchess and then to other appointments about my *pension.* . . .

I hope to get away Thursday night. Believe, and tell the nursery, that I am very anxious to be back with you all.

It is believed that Carnot will be elected—I hope not.

What do you say to the Russian note?

I dine today with Mme. de L[ieven].

[PARIS, *?* 12 *March* 1850.]

The votes of the soldiers are not so bad as is said, but not good. They vote against their officers and like to act with independence. The opinion is that on the whole the elections will be good. Recollect that the elected cannot be worse than those they replace.

I had read the Russian despatch in the original —it is well written and strong.[1] . . .

[PARIS] *Thursday* [*March* 14, 1850].

I intended to write yesterday to calm you on the subject of the socialist elections,[2] but my letter was too late for the post.

[1] This was a despatch from the Russian to the French Government arising out of the British intervention against Greece in favour of Don Pacifico. It was a protest against the abuse of England's maritime power for the purpose of coercing small states. A copy had been transmitted from Paris to London.

[2] The elections took place on Sunday, March 10.

117

THE SECRET OF THE COUP D'ÉTAT

This is a miserable country. Monday and Tuesday morning there was no doubt of the triumph of the moderates, and in consequence legitimists and Orleanists indulged in their party feelings, and especially the first, made all the opposition they could to the government. Towards the middle of the day yesterday, the result of the ballot began to be known and to create some alarm; but late in the afternoon, when the final result was announced, there was a complete consternation. I was at the Club of the Rue de Graucourt when the first news came and you have no notion of the long faces. Auguste tells me that today at the Chamber it seemed as if everything was lost, and your little favourite[1] more so than anybody. The fact is however that in the actual situation of things, it makes no change, for it is only 3 rascals who are replaced by 3 others—only it shows that the opinion that a favourable change had taken place in the dispositions of the Paris population was erroneous. It is said that in the provinces the elections will have been better.

My affair is not yet settled. I hope it will be before the end of the week, but at all events I shall leave this on Monday and think that Villa

[1] Thiers.

BEFORE THE COUP D'ÉTAT

Real will accompany me. . . . I had a note today from Mme. de Lieven ending with these words: "Je veux des conseils: faut-il partir avec vous?"

Flahault to Lord Murray[1]

TULLYALLAN, *Sept.* 7, 1850.

I have read none of the articles on L. P.[2] published since his death. In giving an account of his life, newspaper writers may give the facts more or less exactly, but how can they appreciate the pressure of the circumstances under which L. P. was forced to act? The conduct of his father, the hatred of the Court, the dangers of all sorts that surrounded him on all sides, and forced him to fly his country without a chance of finding a resting-place in any corner of Europe —and later in 1830 the necessity he was in of accepting the crown of his relatives or sharing again the exile their faults had condemned them to.

Politically his death is without any importance, and has produced no effect whatever in France. The President's journey has been as successful as it possibly could be, and his conduct

[1] John Archibald Murray, the well-known Scotch judge, and an old friend of both the Comte and Comtesse de Flahault.
[2] Louis Philippe.

119

and language have been able and approved by everybody; but what will happen nobody can tell, and Morny and Lavalette, who are with me, are as ignorant of it as you and me. . . .

Flahault to Morny

A fair copy of the letter which follows was kept by the sender, so it may be assumed that special importance was attached to it.   There can be little doubt that it was intended for the eyes of the President, and, as will be seen further on, Flahault from time to time adopted this method of giving him the benefit of his advice and of his knowledge of English views in regard to diplomatic questions of the day.

The copy is without date, but the letter was evidently written not long after the death of the ex-King of the French.   The European question alluded to is that which arose in regard to the quarrel between Denmark and the Duchies (Holstein) and the possibility of the intervention of the allied powers therein.   Morny, it appears, had just returned to France, after staying with Flahault in Scotland.

[LONDON, *Oct.* 1850.]

My dear friend,

Is the *Times* report true as to a proposal which has been made to England by the Russian and French Governments for the joint presentation by the three powers of a note to Prussia?[1] It is said that the note demands the punctual execution of the terms of the treaty between Prussia and Denmark relative to the Duchies, and that it contains a threat—in the event of refusal or of the continued non-execution of the treaty—that Silesia will be occupied by Russian and the Rhenish provinces by French troops.

I should myself have thought Russian diplomacy too astute to have made such a proposal to the English Government, for there could be no doubt as to the reply, and this must surely be foreseen. It is not this time a question of Palmerston's opinion, for no single member of an English cabinet, whether Whig or Tory, would lend himself to such a policy. The annihilation of the Duchies would indeed be considered preferable to either of the suggested military occupations.

You know the views I hold as to the Rhenish provinces. I would neither threaten Prussia, nor make propositions to England, but should Prussia fire a single shot I would immediately occupy the

---

[1] In October, 1850, a proposal was made by Russia that she, in conjunction with England and France, should assist Denmark in her dispute with Holstein.

Rhenish provinces. In this event it would be desirable that Russia should occupy Silesia. She would thus be compromised, while she would be prevented from joining forces with Germany, should this country forget her own internal dissensions and attempt to form a united front against the aggression of their common foe. As to England, she would take no action, once the thing was done. To refuse to do anything is quite a different matter from stopping by force of arms a thing which has been done. Awkward consequences may be involved by the mere putting forward of such a proposition as that suggested, for those who object to it are almost bound to oppose its subsequent execution.

In her present condition, financially and politically, England can only carry on a war which is popular, and this country does not attach enough importance to the Rhenish provinces to justify Parliament in voting the taxes which the war would necessitate. If it was a question of Belgium, or in particular of Antwerp, it would be different. As to the personal position of Prince Louis, I do not know of anything which would more tend to consolidate it than such a course of action. I am firmly convinced of two things, that the English Government would neither consent to it in advance, nor declare war in order to prevent it.

I have read Granier de Cassagnac's articles, they are well written, but in my view it would have been still better if he had not written them at all. Let time do its work. The moment will probably come when those who are to-day the most vehemently against the extension of the President's term of office will be the keenest to demand it; and besides there will be this difference:—if the proposal is made now, the Assembly will dictate its conditions to Prince Louis, while towards the autumn of 1851 it will be a case of Prince Louis dictating his conditions to the Assembly. His position is a very strong one, for he has no possible competitor.

M. de Salvandy[1] was extremely well received at Frohsdorff; indeed I hear the same of all their visitors—This is in accordance with the Evangelical maxim which tells us that there is more joy over one sinner who repents than over 99 just men! Poor Salvandy is a ready convert.

The publication of the *Circulaire Barthélemy*[2]

[1] After the death of Louis Philippe on August 26, 1850, Salvandy had paid a visit to the Comte de Chambord at Frohsdorff, in the interest of the "fusion" proposal.

[2] M. de Barthélemy was secretary of the Paris Legitimist Committee. He issued a circular to the provincial committees informing them that

was not intended either by the Comte de Chambord, or by his advisers; it was done without their knowledge, and they were naturally somewhat annoyed. But these people make a habit of discovering the hand of God in everything which occurs, and so they have accepted it! They say that the words used are straightforward and loyal, and that they give, in fact, expression to the feelings and intentions of their leader— "that he is determined never to return to France, except at the call of duty and when his rights are fully recognised"; so they do not regret that the document has been given such publicity. You can rely on the correctness of this information.

I have not yet been to Claremont, nor to Esher, but I intend to do so in a few days.[1] Poor people, how sorely tried they have been!

* Morny to Madame de Flahault

The next three documents are principally concerned with the offer (not elsewhere recorded) to Flahault of the French Ambassadorship in London. A memoralist of the "Monarchie de Juillet" (the

---

their candidate, the Comte de Chambord, was unwilling to submit his claims to a popular vote. This message was published in the French newspapers on September 20, 1850.

[1] No doubt in order to express his condolence on the death of the King of the French.

Marquis de Castellane) tells us that some eighteen years before Flahault greatly desired this post, and that Talleyrand, who then held it, thought that his protégé had tried to oust him. However this may have been, Flahault would not take it now, although both his wife and Morny threw their weight on the side of acceptance, and nine years were to elapse before he was actually installed in London as the representative of the country of his birth.

[PARIS, *Sunday, Feb. 23*, 1851.]

Dear Madame de Flahault,

I have answered part of your political queries by some information which M. de Flahault has no doubt passed on to you, and by sending you the terms of the Constitution.[1] You must now understand what chance the President has got of being legally re-elected. In my opinion he has none, and the solution of the matter must be extra-legal. As you will have perceived, the President's term of office expires before that of the Assembly; and should the existing Assembly not have meanwhile declared the Constitution to be capable of revision, it will conduct the presidential election itself and will see that the existing law

[1] The Revision of the Constitution of 1848 was at this time under discussion.

125

is strictly applied. Thus the Assembly could easily stifle the will of the people by declaring all the votes invalid. So, either the Assembly must declare by a majority of three-quarters of its members that the Constitution can be revised, or else there will be a fight—and one side or the other must be beaten. I do not believe that in our Assembly, where it is hard to obtain even a bare majority, it will ever be possible to find three-quarters of the members in agreement.[1] So the things must be left to chance! My idea is that the Revision having been refused, the Assembly will find itself so unpopular that it will have to disappear—followed by the curses of the country. But in any case it must have a violent ending.

I see that on your side also you are approaching a difficult time, and I own that I am unable to understand how, in view of the composition of the House of Commons and the events which preceded (and indeed caused) the fall of the Whig Ministry, a Tory Ministry could be formed, or at any rate how such a Ministry could last. I should be less astonished at an alliance between

---

[1] Morny was right. Though a majority of the Assembly afterwards (July 19) pronounced in favour of revision, the required proportion was not forthcoming.

Palmerston and the Radicals. I fear that great difficulties may be in store for England, but in spite of the general anxiety, I shall always put my trust in the common sense of the people. I wish I could say as much for my fellow country-men.

So M. de Flahault has refused the London Embassy! Was he wise to do so? If his conscience says "yes," I have nothing more to say. But the more I consider his reasons the less good I think them. First, as regards Palmerston, this no longer counts, so I will not argue about it.[1] I imagine that if it were Lord Aberdeen or any one else his objections would no longer exist. Then, as to his position,—is it not quite different from that of others who have served the late King? Would not his attach-ment to the Emperor and to Queen H.[2] be a sufficient justification for a manifestation of personal devotion to Prince Louis? As to his objection to serve, as he says, under the Republic, this cannot be taken seriously. Cavaignac or Ledru Rollin *were* the Republic, but since the establishment of the Presidency the Republic

[1] Lord John Russell had just resigned, though his resignation was afterwards withdrawn.
[2] Queen Hortense, Morny's mother.

exists only in name—it is an outward form which may well be objected to on account of its instability, but which need no longer be an obstacle to those who prefer a Monarchy; for when all is said and done it is Prince Louis who stands for authority. To him there are no doubt real objections:—his individuality, the memories which he evokes, the hopes to which he gives birth—but it is not these which trouble M. de Flahault, rather the reverse! The Prince greatly regrets his refusal; should he,—in view of the gravity of the situation with a new government, of the great importance of good relations between France and England, and of the fact that it is in his power to render such important services— reconsider it; pray let me know. It would delight the Prince who would then immediately install him at the London Embassy.

Good-bye, dear Madame de Flahault. I don't know whether you will be able to read my infamous handwriting. Believe me yours sincerely and most affectionately,

AUGUSTE.

I close this letter on Monday, February 24th! What a date![1] Please forgive me.

[1] The anniversary of the Revolution three years before.

BEFORE THE COUP D'ÉTAT

* Madame de Flahault to Morny

GROSVENOR SQUARE,
26 *February* [1851]

You are preaching to the converted, my dear
Auguste, but every one must be free to act according to his conscience, and I am unable to influence
M. de Flahault in his intentions. My English
ideas will always make me prefer the country's
good to political considerations, whether of interest
or of sentiment. I believe that the extension of
the President's term of office, under some kind
of monarchical form, is most necessary for the
peace and quiet of France and for her defence
against the foreign intrigues and aggressions
which are sure to come. I yield to no one in
my feelings of affection for the Orléans family,
and in my solicitude for the Duke's unfortunate
children, whom I have known since they were
born. Nevertheless the same constitutional principles which prompted me to urge M. de Flahault
to support the younger branch in 1830 now
move me in a contrary direction, for I hold that
the President has six million more reasons in
his favour than had Louis Philippe when he was
invited by Messrs. Lafayette, Lafitte, Pasquier,
Decaze and Co. to govern the country; nor do

THE SECRET OF THE COUP D'ÉTAT

I think that any one, except those who recognise nothing short of divine right, can legally dispute his right to be at the head of the State.

There is no doubt that were M. de Flahault to follow his inclination, he would not hesitate a moment to serve the Emperor's nephew and heir, but he detests the Republic, and really he has said too much against it to give it now his whole-hearted service. This is the principal difficulty; but in my opinion the question resolves itself into a choice between a government of law and order and the Red Republic, and for my part I hold to the view that it is incumbent on every honest man to support and to strengthen, as far as he can, that form of government which can show the strongest guarantees against anarchy and the socialists.

These are my views, my dear Auguste, and if by giving an example, M. de Flahault were able at this important crisis to bring others to declare themselves in favour of the President, I should regret all the more that he does not consider himself able and willing to help him in the great and good work, which he is carrying out so splendidly.

You, who know M. de Flahault, are aware

how anxious he is that no false construction should be put on his action, and that it should not be thought due to any motives of self-interest. Perhaps time and circumstances may make him less sensitive on this score.

* Morny to Flahault

[PARIS] *Sunday* [? *March 2*, 1851.]

My dear friend,

I am sorry that my letter to Madame de Flahault has displeased you. I had thought the matter over and had come to the conclusion that as regards French feeling towards the Republic you were both of the same mind, but that it was otherwise in regard to the question of taking service under the Prince's government—and I believed that by explaining things to Madame de Flahault I was enlisting the services of a valuable ally in the home circle. But I am no judge of English public feeling, and if it is the case that the suggested post would inconvenience you or that it would adversely affect the excellent position which you enjoy, let there be no further question of it. I have for the Prince a natural attachment, but I hope you will not think it comparable with the affection which I bear towards you. So let us say no more about it.

131

I thought the plan would be useful from his point of view, and agreeable from yours, and that your refusal was only due to scruples which, coming from you, I considered a little exaggerated, and to motives which would not be appreciated here.

I am still very unwell; I was not even able to take part in yesterday's debate. It was a fine debate and one which affords some food for thought. I am much afraid that we are tending towards the "Reds"—the spirit of loyal resignation shown by the Prince, the strict observance of the Constitution, and the general blindness are all taking us straight towards that goal.

It is known here that you were offered the London Embassy and that you have refused it. Do not be concerned that the news has leaked out. If you are not, I shall not mind, for it might serve later on to enable you to accept some other post at some other time.

It is true that we are going to draw lots with M. de Bauffremont for the two Italian pictures which, with the panels, are at the Pantechnicon. Will you complete the affair with M. Harcourt, and give him whichever he may win? This is the outcome of a deal which I made with his

father-in-law, M. Leroux.[1] As for my paintings
on wood, you can send them over at the same
time as your silver. Have you no answer as to
the silver refinery? P . . . is very anxious to
know. I don't know what to say about English
affairs—Europe seems to me to have a fit of the
sulks. God knows what mess we shall have to
swallow in 1852!

What a jade of a horse you have sent me. If
I were to buy a pair in France, do you think he[2]
would take it back?

Good-bye, dear friend. I embrace you tenderly.
When are you likely to come over?   **A.**

Flahault to Madame de Flahault

In Paris during the spring of 1851 things were
rapidly advancing towards the crisis. In England
everybody was absorbed in the Great Exhibition,
which was just about to be opened. Flahault's
letters show how the various parties were working:
some for the *Revision* of the Constitution in such
a way as to secure the re-election of the President,
some for the *prolongation* of his term of office in

---

[1] Morny's dealings in pictures were numerous. It would seem that
his collection had been sent to England with a view to sale, and that
part of it was temporarily hung on the walls of Flahault's London
house (see p. 331).

[2] *I.e.* the vendor.

order to avoid the necessity of his re-election, and others for the *fusion* of the ambitions of the various royalist claimants into one person. It is curious to find that Changarnier, who had been summarily ejected by the President at the beginning of the year from his position as Commander-in-Chief, was nevertheless received as the guest of honour at a dinner party given by Princess de Lieven, but Henry Greville tells us that Madame de Lieven's salon was always neutral territory.

Flahault appears to have been, as always, well received on all sides, for he was not as yet generally identified with the *parti Élysée*.

He returned to England about the middle of May. It would seem that Morny was thinking of accompanying him. We do not know whether he did so, but if he came to England it was not for long, for the idea of a *coup d'état* had come to be recognised as inevitable, and Morny with his friends was soon to work out the details by which it was to be accomplished.

[PARIS] *April* 11 [1851].

I have just got your two letters of yesterday with your account of the wonders of the Great Exhibition—I hope it may succeed but shall be astonished if it does.

BEFORE THE COUP D'ÉTAT

I must answer you about Cassiobury. I am quite surprised that you should have known nothing of Lady E.;[1] even abroad she has made a noise and astonished [*sic*]. Carlsbad was full of stories about her. I don't think it signifies for you who are respectable enough not to mind it, but for Georgina I beg that on no account you will take her there. She may sham an indisposition. . . .

I cannot tell you how amused I am with the speed at which your imagination travels as to the action of the German powers. . . .

[PARIS]
Sunday morning [20 April 1851].

I have to thank you for two letters, one received at Brussels, the other here. . . .

Everything here is tranquil at this moment from the Chamber having given itself Easter holidays. However, the anxiety as to the future is very great and likely to increase daily. It is true as you heard that Guizot, Duchâtel, D. de Noailles, de Levis, etc., etc., have agreed to the *fusion*, and have all subscribed, some 30 thousand francs, others 10, to purchase the *Assemblée Nationale* in order to support that cause. They

[1] Essex.

135

know that this measure is not approved of at Esher and also at Claremont,[1] but they don't care, and consider that those who do so, don't understand their own interest nor that of the country and are led in this conduct by the wronghead [*sic*] and passion of Thiers and Lasteyrie, whom they abuse in not very measured language.

Their argument is this:—The abdication of the King has put an end to the Orléans dynasty. What one revolution had done another has destroyed. It is vain to talk of replacing the Ct. de Paris on the throne as the heir of Louis Philippe; and it could only be by the restoration of the principle of legitimacy and as successor of Henry V., or in case of the latter's death, that he could, by becoming the legitimate heir and obtaining the support of the whole monarchical party, hope to be restored to his rights. In the meanwhile, they say that the only thing possible is to maintain what exists, and that every effort must be made to prolong the powers of the President, and this they are prepared to do. However, they admit that it cannot be done in a legal manner, but as a *coup d'état* by the Assembly, and how that is to be achieved— Thiers and the pure Orleanists and the Mountain

[1] *I.e.* by the Duchesse d'Orléans or by Queen Marie Amélie.

COMTE DE MORNY

(From a daguerreotype, c. 1849)

and Cavaignac party opposing it—I am at a loss to understand.

I have seen Broglie, who is the most honest man of this country. He has been very useful in constructing the present ministry. He begged to be remembered to you and Emily, and by her to Ld. L.[1]

To give you an idea of my activity. I called yesterday first to write my name for the President, then on Mmes. de Noailles, de Girardin, on Carbonel, Guizot, Mmes. de Lobau, de Massa, de Caraman, Duchâtel and Richard Metternich. I have written them in this confused order because I did not find them at home and wished to separate them from those I saw, which were Mme. de Lieven, who received me *à bras ouverts*, but is furious because I refused to go to her Sunday soirées. Being in the house I saw also Ly. Sandwich. Then I went to Broglie, with whom I had a good long talk. Guizot I met at Mme. de L. I then went in the evening to Passy, where I found nothing but the family and Rémusat, who looks a little sheepish. I dine there to-day, to-morrow at Lady Sandwich's, and Wednesday at Mme. de Lieven's with Changarnier, Broglie, Duchâtel and G.

[1] Lord Lansdowne.

139

THE SECRET OF THE COUP D'ÉTAT

Poor Excelmans went to the station to meet me, but was too late, he called on me Friday night. His baton[1] has made him quite young again.

Now that I have given you a detailed account of myself, I must add that this activity is quite odious to me, but it would appear strange to come to Paris to pass one's day at home *en robe de Chambre;*—and yet if I did I should have Auguste for companion for he is unwell, and since my arrival has not left his room and hardly his bed.

[PARIS] *Thursday* [*24 April* 1851].

My dinner yesterday went off very well. The Pss.[2] had asked the Ashleys, St. Aulaires, Molé, Guizot, Changarnier, D. de Noailles. It was not exactly amusing but not uninteresting. Changarnier said that the *revision* would be proposed by the Government, but if not by the Government, by some one of the opposition; that it was a question that must be disposed of, but that once disposed of,—whether adopted or rejected, —the actual agitation would cease. Molé said that a month ago Duvergier d'Hauranne meant to propose it, but that he had given up that intention.

[1] He had been made a Marshal in 1849   [2] de Lieven.

BEFORE THE COUP D'ÉTAT

I think it very cross and absurd of the possessors of season tickets to make such a piece of work about the Queen's visit to the Exhibition and to grudge H.M. those few hours.[1] . . .

Flahault to Lady Shelburne

[PARIS] *Thursday [April 24, 1851].*

My dear Emily,

I dined yesterday with Madame de Lieven to meet the St. Aulaires, Ashleys, Molé, Guizot, Changarnier and the Duc de Noailles. Just conceive, the adulation of General Changarnier is such that it was to him she gave her arm when we went in to dinner! He seemed to me rather downcast. He wears a deceitful expression and his manners are common. We had there the *general staff* of the *Fusion* party. Did you know that this party refuses to accept the Duchess of Orléans as Regent? They describe her nomination for that post as an abortive revolutionary scheme![2] The Duc de Nemours is the person they look upon as Regent. . . . Auguste is better.

[1] The Prince Consort had insisted that, to give more room, the holders of season tickets should be excluded from the opening ceremony of the Exhibition, but he was eventually persuaded by Lord Granville to withdraw the embargo (Henry Greville, *Diary*).

[2] *Une tentative révolutionnaire avortée.*

141

THE SECRET OF THE COUP D'ÉTAT

* Louis Napoleon to Flahault

ÉLYSÉE NATIONALE, 24 *April* 1851.

My dear General,

I am very sorry that up to now indisposition has prevented me from receiving you, and I hasten to assure you once more of my affection.

So please come and dine on Friday next at three o'clock. I should be glad to have a talk with you.

Believe me with great esteem yours,

LOUIS NAPOLÉON B.

Flahault to Madame de Flahault

[PARIS, *Friday, April 25,* 1851.]

I have just received your letter of yesterday which frightened me, being dated by mistake April 29. . . .

I found last night on coming home a note which I here copy:

Mon cher Général,

Je suis bien fâché qu'une indisposition m'avait empêché jusqu'à ce jour de vous recevoir, et il me tarde de vous renouveler l'assurance de mes senti-mens affectueux. Venez donc dîner ce Vendredi à trois heures. Je serai heureux de causer avec vous.

Croyez à ma haute estime.

LOUIS NAPOLÉON B.

It is kind and well expressed—I am going there and have time for little more.

Last night I went with Ld. and Ly. Ashley to see *Valerie*. Nothing can be more disgusting. In short, with my *souvenirs*, I feel nothing but disappointment at a theatre.

I dine to-night at Passy.

There is a letter in this day's *Constitutionnel* which I beg you to read and tell me what you think of it.

[PARIS] *Sunday [April 27, 1851].*

You don't mention the day of the Queen's concert, therefore I cannot answer you as to my return. . . .

My visit was very agreeable. It is impossible to be more kind and good-natured and to have received better my reasons for not accepting what he had proposed.[1] I must reserve the details of our conversation till we meet.

As I was going, he recalled me and said, "I shall ask you to allow me to present to you an old acquaintance. Do you remember a coachman named Florenton whom you sent to my Mother with two horses from Geneva?[2] Well, he is

[1] The London ambassadorship.

[2] Louis Napoleon is here referring to Flahault's attempt, in August, 1815, to establish himself with Queen Hortense in Switzerland after the fall of Napoleon (see Introduction, p. 56.)

still in my service and I shall be glad to present him to you." That shows a good heart. . . .

[PARIS] Friday [MAY 2, 1851].

I have got your two letters of yesterday, and although I never had the slightest doubt of the thing going off quietly,[1] I am delighted that you found all so convenient and were so well placed.

I read your letter to Auguste and M. Rouher, which last said it was heartrending to bring back one's thoughts upon this unfortunate country. My hand and stiff neck make writing much too painful to enter at length on this fatal subject, even if the post were a safe means of communication; but when we meet, which will be ere long, I will give you very disquieting details. . . . I dine to-day at the President's.

[PARIS, Saturday] May 3 [1851].

I am not at all sick of your writing, but heartily so of <i>mine</i> for I do it very uncomfortably! . . .

The P. was amazed and much pleased with your account of the opening of the Exhibition. I dined there with Pss. Mathilde, Pr. and Pss. Furstenberg, Hertford, Ld. and Ly. Ely, Ly. Glengall, Mrs. Anson, Pembroke, Gen. and Mme.

---

[1] The opening of the Great Exhibition in London.

Chasseloup Laubat (she is remarried to her brother-in-law), Gl. Baraguay d'Illers (the successor of Changarnier), etc., etc., etc.—40 people. I was surprised for he had told me that he would ask me *en petit comité*. He was very amiable and kind to me, and I stayed to talk with him and smoke a cigarette, after everybody was gone. He appears to me to understand perfectly his position.

I forgot to mention that I was at Molé's Thursday night for the *signature du contrat*.[1] All Paris was there.

[PARIS] *Monday* [*May 5*, 1851].

Yesterday was very rainy and cold and of a nature to calm all socialists, who could only get wet in common with everybody. There was, however, a good number singing and hollowing all night in the Champs Elysées.

I am now going to the *cérémonie funèbre* for the anniversary of the 5th May[2] at the Invalides. . . . Auguste wants to know if, in case he could accompany me on my return, you could make up a bed for him for 3 days?

[1] Molé's granddaughter, Mlle. de Champlâtreux, was about to marry the eldest son of the Duc de Noailles, a match which provoked much interest in Paris.

[2] The death of Napoleon I.

THE SECRET OF THE COUP D'ÉTAT

[PARIS] *Friday* [*May* 9, 1851].

I am thinking seriously of my departure. . . .
I doubt much Auguste's coming with me, but
if he does I will not have you leave your room,
and am sure it would put him in despair. I
could sleep in that room and dress in your
dressing-room.

I know nothing about Pss. Mathilde's doings.
I met her at the P's, when she was very amiable
and kind, but have not found her at home, though
I have called twice.

Have you read the articles in the *Débats*
against the *fusion?* They have produced a
great effect and given great offence to G[uizot]
D[uchâtel] and Co. . . .

You are an admirable correspondent, and I
should be a better one did writing not make my
neck and head very painful.

[PARIS] *Monday* [? *May* 12, 1851].

I am sorry that I am not in London to-day to
go to the concert of H.M., but I had accepted
a dinner at Psse. Mathilde's.[1]

With regard to levées and drawing-rooms, I
have explained to Pce. Albert himself the reasons

[1] He dined with her on Tuesday, May 13, in company with Morny,
Exelmans, and others (cf. Viel-Castel's *Memoirs*.)

146

which prevent my having the honour of attending them. I do not want to go there as an Englishman, nor do I wish to go with the representative of the Republic.

What a sorry set of my countrymen you have met at the Exhibition!

I don't think that Auguste would consent to disturb either you or me; therefore, if he comes, a bed in the library would be the best arrangement, but I still doubt his coming.

I have had a long talk with the P. and found him full of sense, instruction, and firmness in his views. There is a great move all over the country in favour of his *prolongation*.[1] At Lyons many houses open for people to sign petitions in favour of it. Thiers declares himself his enemy, and some time ago intended to establish a Directory of which he would be the head and four generals members. It is said, however, that since a journey he has made lately in the Department du Nord and some letters he has received from the Seine-Infèrieure (for which he is Deputy) his language is much modified.

I went this morning to St. Philippe du Roule to the marriage of young Le Hon with Mlle.

---

[1] The *revision* of the Constitution involving the *prolongation des pouvoirs présidentiels* became in the summer of 1851 a burning question.

Mosselmann, who is a very nice girl.   Barrot was there, but I did not speak to him.

I am sorry that the young Princes[1] in England do themselves a good deal of harm by the inconsiderate manner and contradictory language in which they express themselves upon the *fusion*, according to the opinion of the person to whom they write.

. . . Mad. de Lieven and Lady Palmerston are reconciled.

[1] Louis Philippe's sons, the duc de Nemours and the prince de Joinville.

II

THE COUP D'ÉTAT

(NOVEMBER AND DECEMBER, 1851)

II

HISTORIANS of the Second Republic have been at pains to point out that only five persons—Morny, St. Arnaud, Persigny, Maupas and the President's confidential secretary Mocquard—shared with Louis Napoleon the secret of the *coup d'état*. The letters which follow show that Flahault's name must be added to this list. It is not easy to say precisely at what period he became privy to the plot, but there is every reason to suppose that Morny during the summer of 1851 had kept him informed of all that had been passing, and that when he came over to Paris in the early part of November, it was for the express purpose of assisting in the events which had been arranged to take place before the end of that month. As he himself explains to his daughter, Lady Shelburne, just after the event, he had at first cherished the hope that the change could be effected with the approval or assistance of the majority of the

151

Assembly, instead of being (as it had to be in the end) the work of the Executive in defiance of the Legislative authority.

The date, as we know, had been several times altered. September or October had originally been suggested, and November 20 was changed to November 25, and again to December 2. When Flahault left England he evidently thought that all would be comfortably over in a few weeks, for he had promised—somewhat rashly as it turned out—to rejoin his family by the end of November.

He appears to have arrived in Paris a few days after the reassembling of the Chamber on November 4, and had not long to wait for the opening moves in the final conflict between Louis Napoleon and the Assembly.

The President began by asking the legislature to repeal the Electoral Law of May 31, which they had themselves passed a little more than a year before with his full concurrence. The Act had been one which considerably curtailed the suffrage. The President's proposal was therefore, as it was intended to be, a popular one outside the Chamber; and its defeat in a house of over 700 by a majority of 7 on November 13 merely served to enhance his position and to bring over some of the waverers to his side.

THE COUP D'ÉTAT

Next came the famous *Proposition des Questeurs* —an attempt by the Assembly, acting through its officials, to regain the final control of the Army, which, in spite of decrees to the contrary, had been allowed for all practical purposes to pass into the hands of the Executive. The President's immediate response to this proposal was to order the old decrees to be destroyed wherever they might be found. A few days afterwards (November 17) the Chamber proceeded to discuss and to vote upon the proposal, when (apparently to the general surprise) it was defeated by a large majority.

The Chamber was thus discredited and powerless, and the inner circle of the *Partie d'Élysée* were able to select what seemed the most auspicious day —the anniversary of Austerlitz—for the *coup*, for which we now learn the final arrangements had been made on Thursday, November 27.

As may be gathered from the correspondence, Flahault, after assisting on the Consultative Commission, appointed by the President to decide on questions connected with the new form of government, eventually left Paris on December 25. After two days in London he rejoined his family at Bowood, where they were spending Christmas with Lord Lansdowne, at this time President of the Council.

THE SECRET OF THE COUP D'ÉTAT

Lord John Russell was Prime Minister, and I have inserted a few letters from unpublished Lansdowne Papers which are of interest as throwing fresh light on the circumstances of the replacement of Lord Palmerston by Lord Granville as Foreign Secretary.

Flahault to Madame de Flahault

CHAMPS ÉLYSÉES,
Thursday [*November* 6, 1851].

My letter from Boulogne has told you of my miseries. However, I got here last night at 12 o'clock. Auguste was out, so I went to bed and was awoke by him a little after one, when, after shaking hands, I sent him off. We have this morning breakfasted together and had a long talk; from which I find that I was right in most things though not in all. I made my journey with a young Englishman who was anything but favourable to the changes that have taken place in this country and was rather funny in many things he said.

[PARIS] *Tuesday* [*November* 11, 1851].

You can have no idea of the confusion both in the things and minds of the people here. What will come of it God only knows, but little good I suspect.

THE COUP D'ÉTAT

I am not very famous to-day, my sickness having left me very bilious. Auguste's levées are more numerous than ever. We breakfasted with the room quite full, Rouher, Boilay, etc., etc., etc., and the drawing-room full of people waiting. It is a country of beggars.

I hear that owing to Palmerston's supposed favour to the refugees of all nations, the English are extremely unpopular.[1] Send my letters to Emily with my love. . . .

[PARIS] *Thursday* [*November* 13, 1851].

Things are getting very hot here, and I should be astonished if it could go on much longer without a conflict between the powers of the State. The President has given the order to tear down in all the barracks the order of the Constituent Assembly to the troops to obey the requisitions of the Assembly. This, in answer to the proposition of the Questors, must bring matters to an issue. You shall hear if anything takes place. I am now going to the President. . . .

What is to be done with the pattern of a stocking Charlotte has given Greystone?

[1] Kossuth had come to England towards the end of October and Palmerston had insisted on receiving him.

THE SECRET OF THE COUP D'ÉTAT

Lady Shelburne to Georgine de Flahault

BOWOOD, *Nov.* 14 [1851].

I return you Papa's letter with many thanks. They seem to be in a pretty kettle of fish at Paris, and I doubt it ending peaceably.

I went yesterday to Calne. . . . Lady Pembroke and Lady Bruce were full of a report put about I believe by Maussion (at least *he* had told Ly. Dunmore) that Papa was gone over to Paris to be Prime Minister and help the President out of his difficulties! I said that I had heard from him that morning and that he had announced his return for the 28th, and that tho' ministries did not last long in France, I thought that would be even shorter than the average. Ly. Pembroke said she had never for an instant believed it, that she was sure he was much too wise, etc., etc. . . .

Flahault to Madame de Flahault

[PARIS] *Friday* [*November* 14], 1851.

You will have seen this day the vote of last night. A majority of 7 on a question of that importance proposed by Government is too insignificant to be worth anything. The law of the 31st of May cannot remain the law for the elec-

tions of 1852. They say that Molé and Thiers
were very downcast at the end of the sitting.
Now comes Vitet's report on the Questors proposition. My opinion is that it will be rejected;
but I hope that the President will state firmly to
the Assembly that he will never recognise its
right to give direct orders to Generals or troops,
and declare that it is by his personal order that
the decree of the Constituent Assembly has been
destroyed in the barracks. . . . It is perfectly
true that Cavaignac is going to marry a daughter
of the elder brother of Mathilde's husband. She
is 16 and Cavaignac 50!

Lady Shelburne to Madame de Flahault

BOWOOD, *Sunday* [*November* 16, 1851].

I return you Papa's letter with many thanks.
One is glad to have some accts. one can rely on
in the midst of all the conflicting reports the
newspapers are full of.

You know what my feelings about little Thiers
have long been, and will not therefore suspect
me of partiality towards him, but I can quite
understand such men as M. Molé, and the more
respectable men of the moderate party, feeling
great resentment at being called upon to repeal
what they were asked to vote little more than a

year ago,[1] merely because it serves the President's personal views. It may not be politic to refuse to do so in the present state of the country, but I can imagine their being angry, and my own impression is that if the President had allowed things to take their course, tho' he might not have had the number of votes required by the Constitution, still he would have been re-elected by so large a majority that any other candidate would have been impossible, and at least his reputation for consistency and good faith would not have suffered.

Flahault to Madame de Flahault

[PARIS] *Sunday* [16th *November*, 1851].

You are an invaluable correspondent, and I wish my hand enabled me to show myself worthy of you. However, I do my best. . . . I wish in all your commissions you would always fix the price.

I have sent your letter to the Montagnes Russes. Mme. Toussaint will buy your stockings, *camisoles*, order your cap, and get patterns of stuff for your gown. With regard to the making of it, she says that Palmyre has still an establish-

[1] *I.e.* the Electoral Law of May 31, 1850.

ment *dirigé par un successeur*, but if you liked
Mme. Delessert or Mme. le H[on] to order it,
either would do it with pleasure. But I must
tell you that the latter has a considerable number
of *volants;* I think I counted 9 the other night
in thinking of your gown. . . . In what you have
to order, don't forget the state of the King of
Hanover's health.[1] . . .

[PARIS] *Tuesday* [*November* 18], 1851.

You know by this time the miserable *décon-
fiture* of the Assembly.[2] Changarnier, Thiers and
Co. were not prepared for it, but, on the contrary,
anticipated a triumph, and had planned the *mise
en accusation* of the President and the permanence
of the Assembly. Auguste, on hearing it, ran to
the Élysée to apprise him of it and to ask the
Minister of War to prepare for resistance. It
would have ended in the destruction of the Assembly, all Paris would have applauded and the
funds risen 10 fr. %. However, it is as well as
it is, and now we must see what profit can be
made of it. I saw Molé yesterday, and I think
he lamented much his late campaign with Thiers.

[1] He died on Tuesday, November 18.
[2] The *Proposition des Questeurs* had been defeated in the Assembly
the previous day by 408 votes to 300.

Everybody abuses the latter and you may see what a poor figure he made yesterday. The President is particularly kind to me. I went there last night; there were many people and many enquiries for you. Princess Mathilde was there and asked me to fix a day for dining with her; it is to be Thursday.

. . . Tell Lord Lansdowne that there is a beautiful carpet which was ordered for the Grande Galerie of the Palais Royal—never used, but which will go cheap—66 feet by 28 French measure.

I dined yesterday at Lutheroth's with the Bathyanys. She is as handsome and he as gentlemanlike as ever. Anything than favourable to Pulsky. He has seen and known Mme. de Beck, sent to him as an agent by Kossuth, and he thinks (though he is not certain) under that name. He thinks she has been harshly treated.

[PARIS] *Wednesday* 19 [*November* 1851].

I shall order your gown the moment that you send back the pattern, but I warn you that the King of Hanover is as ill as possible and that Baron Stockhausen, who I saw to-day expects every day to hear of his demise.[1] . . . Auguste is not well to-day owing to the agitation of the

[1] He had died the previous day.

last 8 days. Mme. de Lieven I have often seen; she is quite Presidential, and I believe in a few days everybody will be the same. You can have no idea how all the Parliament men have *l'oreille basse*. I hear that Thiers is furious against everybody; he is said to be ill—his tongue again covered with *aphthes*. *Il est puni par où il a pêché.* . . . Who do you think made his appearance here yesterday?—poor Dehuir! He says that everybody at Vienna is for the President. I went to-day to see the "Grossaltheit." She is still all for Thiers and Changarnier. . . . I can conceive no greater shame for a daughter of an English Duke than marrying on these terms.[1] There are many who are sorry for the vote of Monday and would have preferred a contrary one, because it would have produced a *coup d'état* against the Assembly; but they don't consider that it would have been directed against the party of order and would have separated the President from all the men who compose it. If such a measure is to be taken, it must be on an occasion where the President and the majority will be *d'accord*, and that is not impossible.

[1] An allusion to the marriage of Lady Augusta Gordon Lennox, daughter of the Duke of Richmond, to Prince Edward of Saxe Weimar which took place a few days later. She was at the outset not recognised at Court as a Princess but was officially called Countess Dornberg.

THE SECRET OF THE COUP D'ÉTAT

I have had this morning a long conversation with Dupin, who desires to be kindly remembered to you. Love to all. You will receive from Walewsky a parcel of seeds. Send them to Whylock. I shall bring 31 rose trees with me; it is better than grafts.

Lady Shelburne to Madame de Flahault

BOWOOD, *Thursday* [*November* 1851].

I give this to Ld. Lansdowne who sleeps in town tonight to be ready for the Council at Windsor to-morrow. Papa must be very much disgusted with the state of things at Paris and Auguste's breakfasts will not tend to increase his good opinion of public men there. I wish I could get up a little enthusiasm for any party, *mais j'ai beau faire*, it won't come!

We are invited to Panshanger on the 9th.[1] . . . Lord Lansdowne goes to town for Cabinets on the last day of this month, they will take a week or ten days. . . . We shall certainly go up a few days before we are due at Panshanger, by that time I hope Papa will be come back. . . .

---

[1] The ladies of Flahault's family were all at Panshanger from the 9th to the 15th December and kept Henry Greville, who was their fellow-guest, well informed as to the progress of events in Paris (H. Greville, *Diary*).

THE COUP D'ÉTAT

Flahault to Madame de Flahault

PARIS, [*Sunday*] *November* 23.[1]

Your conversation with the radical M. is very funny. Entre nous his *last alternative* will be the one followed and that ere long. . . .

I am very much solicited to prolong my stay here but I shall set out in the course of next week. However tell Georgy not to be too angry if I don't arrive on the 27th. I assure you that notwithstanding the *cara patria* I long to be with you again.

The book has arrived and Auguste who is enchanted with it sends you 1000 thanks.

[PARIS, *Monday*] *November* 24.[2]

I dined last night at Passy and after dinner heard M. Guttman play on the pianoforte. He is an *élève* of Chopin, who was sent once to give Emily some lessons. He was then young and raw, but is now a most admirable performer. Today I dine at the Rothschilds whom I have not yet seen.

I hope you have read the *Constitutionnel* of this day. The article on the Assembly[3] is violent

---

[1] Postmark Nov. 23, 1851.　　　[2] Postmark Nov. 24, 1851.

[3] *Les deux Dictatures*, in which Granier de Cassagnac charged the Assembly with a plot to oust the President.

and I should not be astonished if Granier de
C[assagnac] was cited to the bar. I am told that
he is prepared with his proofs and will, if called
upon, quote Molé as his informer. You will see
that he (Molé) is indicated as having apprized the
President of the plots made against him. The
fact is that things are getting too hot not to
catch fire soon—I should say even very soon.
The Assembly is a disgusting set of *intriguants*.
I have seen d'Haubersaert who is just come from
Duchâtel and says that he is perfectly reasonable.
D'Haubersaert is well and in better spirits.
Entre nous he tells me that he (Duchâtel) and
Montalivet were much grieved with the reception
they met with at Claremont. The Queen and
Royal Family spoke to them of nothing but *la
pluie et le beau temps*. Thiers and Lasteyrie have
absorbed all their confidence. . . .

You will probably hear of a sort of row which
took place yesterday at the Louvre at the ceremony of the distribution of the medals of the
Great Exhibition. It was nothing more than an
irruption of the public into the hall, owing to the
Minister of Commerce not having apprized the
Prefet de Police and therefore no measures of
precaution had been taken and no agents ordered;
but the President was not ill received. However

he was obliged to retire, the crowd being so dense that the ceremony could not have taken place.

[PARIS] *Wednesday* [? *November 26*].

I always forgot to tell you of my astonishment the day I dined at Princess Mathilde's, to find established as *dame de compagnie* in the place of the old German Baroness—who do you think?— Mme. Desprey who preceded Mlle. Luzy at the poor Mme. de Praslin's.[1] What a choice! but so is everything here. The level has become disgustingly low.

I wish I had known you were going to Esher in time, for I should have written you a letter you might have shown. It is impossible to play a more foolish game than that lady.[2] She is losing entirely the prospects of her son. . . . I dine today at the President's with Lady Douglas, who I hear goes to Germany immediately. Things are getting worse and worse here every day. . . . I hear that the Army is very well disposed.

[1] A few years before, Parisian society had been greatly moved by the murder of the Duchesse de Praslin and the subsequent suicide of her husband. Though the double tragedy was never cleared up, it was generally believed to have been the outcome of an illicit attachment between the Duke and Mlle. Deluzy-Desportes, who was at the time governess to his children.

[2] The Duchess of Orléans.

THE SECRET OF THE COUP D'ÉTAT

[PARIS] *Sunday* [*November* 30].[1]

What you have perceived in Belgrave Square is quite correct and I hope that the lady you saw the other day[2] will have the good sense to remain quiet. . . . The agitation one lives in here would have suited me very well in my youth, but does so very ill now—and yet it can only go on *crescendo*. The old chiefs of the Majority are every day losing ground, and I don't suppose that Broglie and Molé could command a dozen votes. It would be idle to think of combining anything with them. If they and Changarnier had stuck to the President they would have been masters of the country—now they are nothing. You have been misinformed about the Artillery; it is as well disposed as the Infantry and Cavalry—all that requires much more to be calmed than excited. The Assembly is every day falling more into discredit—It is in short in a state of dissolution.

[PARIS] *Monday* [1 *December*].

. . . To-morrow we shall know more of what you heard in Belgrave Square and I hope to tell

---

[1] Postmark Nov. 30, 1851.

[2] The Duchess of Orléans. It would seem from this passage and the succeeding extract, that some one in the Belgrave Square had got an inkling of the events which were in preparation in Paris

you of my return. . . . I dined yesterday at
Mme. de Vatey. We were 10, amongst which
2 deputies and 1 Colonel (a very handsome
military looking man) when the following conversation took place. I must begin by saying
that somebody had mentioned that, a fortnight
ago, two regiments returning from a review and
passing before the Chamber, had on purpose
bousculéd a knot of representatives who were
standing on the *trottoirs*. One of the two deputies
at dinner complained of this, when the Colonel
who did not know his quality said:—

"Que voulez-vous, c'est l'esprit de nos soldats.
Nous n'aimons pas les bavards, et au lieu de les
bousculer nous aurions préférés les jeter dans la
Seine."

(Deputy.) "Mais permettez, Colonel, j'ai l'honneur d'être député, et ce que vous dites-là ne serait
pas aussi facile que vous voulez bien le croire."

(Colonel.) "Monsieur, je vous demande bien
pardon. Je ne savais pas que vous étiez député,
sans quoi je ne me serais pas permis de dire une
chose qui a pu vous être désagréable. Mais
enfin c'est dit, et tout ce que je puis ajouter, c'est
que j'espère que vous savez nager!"

The *esprit réactionnaire* is pushed to that
degree that the other day an Englishman was

black-balled at the Club because his name was Gladstone.

* Louis Napoleon to Flahault

Both the notes from Louis Napoleon which follow, are written on plain paper of the same kind. They were found together amongst the Flahault papers. The wording of the first, addressed to Flahault, indicates that it was despatched from the Elysée after the final gathering of the conspirators had broken up, in the small hours of the morning of the *Deux Décembre*. The second note was probably sent to Morny at the same time; it must refer to the circulars by means of which the departmental prefects were to be apprised of the *coup d'état*. They were sent out according to Véron (*Mémoires d'un bourgeois de Paris*, p. 365) by telegraph on December the 2nd. Flahault was staying with Morny at this time, and no doubt kept both letters as a memento of a somewhat memorable occasion.

ÉLYSÉE NATIONALE, *December 2, 1851.*

My dear General,

I should be very glad to have your company on horseback this morning about eight o'clock.

THE COUP D'ÉTAT

Please accept the assurance of my sincerest esteem.   LOUIS NAPOLÉON B.

Monsieur le Général Flahault,
    at M. de Morny's,
        Champs Élysées.
From the President of the Republic.

* Louis Napoleon to Morny

My dear Morny,

Don't forget to bring me the circulars at one o'clock.—Ever yours,   L. N. B.

Confidential.

Monsieur de Morny, Champs Élysées.
From the President of the Republic.

Flahault to Madame de Flahault

[PARIS] *Tuesday,* 7 ock. A.M. [*Dec.* 2, 1851].[1]

I am just returned from the other side of the Pont de la Concorde, where I accompanied Auguste on his way to the Ministère de l'Intérieur, of which he is gone to take possession. The Chamber is occupied and surrounded with troops, and having passed before Gen. Changarnier's house I saw it full of *sergents de ville* and *Gendarmes mobiles* who were arresting him.

[1] Postmark Dec. 2, 1851.

169

There are a good many besides who are to be arrested. The troops hate the Assembly and are well disposed for the President. There may be partial struggles, but I believe there can be no doubt of the success at Paris. The President has asked me to accompany him on horseback and lends me a horse. If there is anything new in the course of the day I will write, and I have told Auguste to send you a telegraphic message.

Morny to Madame de Flahault

Morny made constant use of the telegraph during the days succeeding the *coup d'état*. The "Electric Telegraph" between France and England had only been opened three weeks previously (November 13). His telegrams to Madame de Flahault were thus amongst the first to be transmitted across the Channel.

Telegram

Received at 11.10 A.M. Tuesday 2nd December

South-Eastern Railway. Electric Telegraph.
From: M. de Morny, Minister of the Interior.

To: Countess Flahault, Grosvenor Square, London.

The Assembly is dissolved. The President of the Republic makes an appeal to the country.

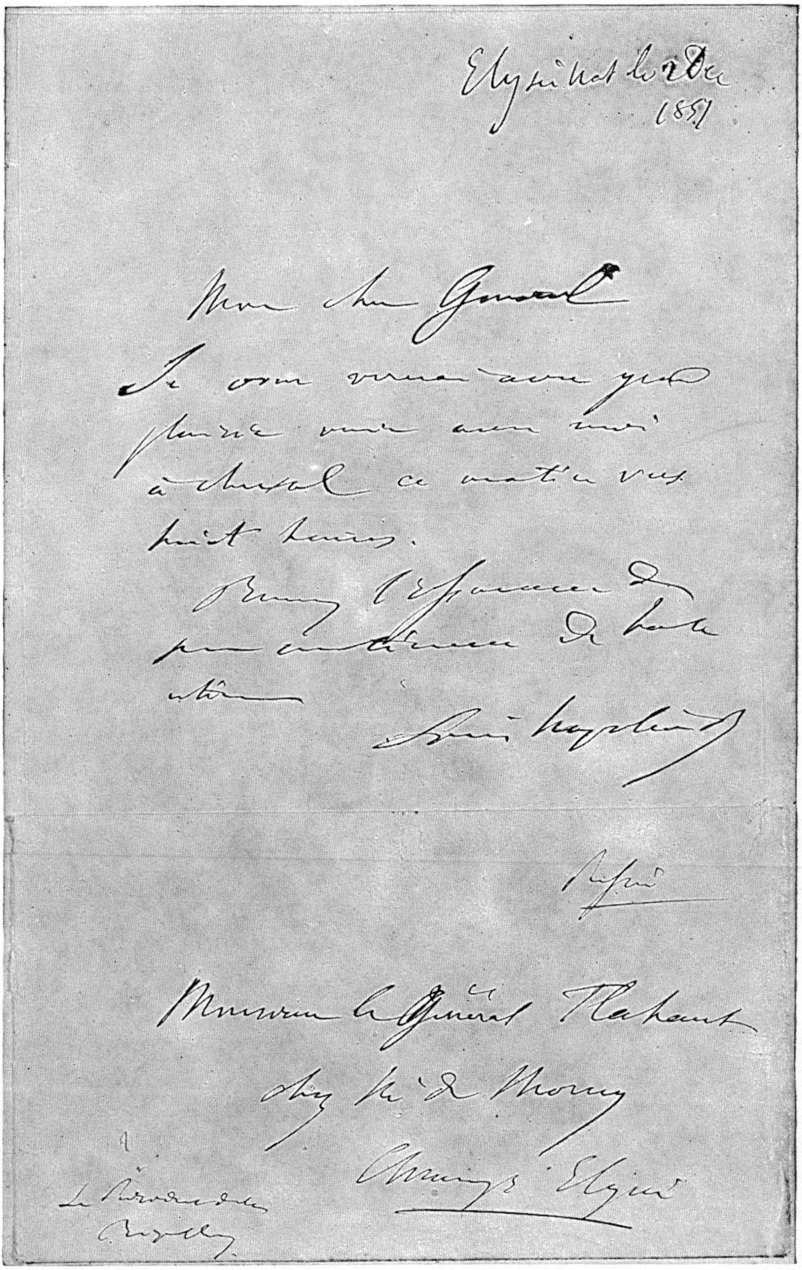

Élysée National le 2 Dec
1851

Mon cher Général

Je vous verrai avec grand
plaisir venir avec moi
à cheval ce matin vers
huit heures.

Recevez l'assurance de
[illegible] de haute
estime

Louis Napoléon

Pressé

Monsieur le Général Flahaut
chez M. de Morny
Champs Élysées

NOTE FROM PRINCE LOUIS NAPOLEON
TO COMTE DE FLAHAULT

THE COUP D'ÉTAT

Flahault to Madame de Flahault

[PARIS] *Wednesday morning*, 9 *o'clock* [*Dec.* 3, 1851].

Yesterday was an eventful and anxious day, not only on account of the uncertainty of the turn things would take, but also on account of those that had to be executed: for it is not without regret that one begins by arresting respectable men whose only fault is being political enemies [*sic*]. However, such was the decision, and when I tell you that since last Thursday [1] all that has been done was resolved upon, you may conceive that those informed must have felt some anxiety. These only were Auguste, St. Arnaud, Maupas (I believe Persigny), and myself, and never was secret better kept and plan better executed.

Auguste has been heroic; nothing can exceed his courage, firmness, good sense, prudence, calm, good humour, gentleness and tact during all that was going on, and at the same time so simple and total absence of vanity and conceit. Those who love him may be proud of him.

Things are going on as well as one can wish and now appear quite simple and easy, but I assure you that when we got up at 5 o'clock and

[1] November 27.

173

went to the Assembly at the moment it was being occupied, it was anything but *rassurant.* The people look perfectly satisfied, they are Bonapartist and Republican. I have refused everything that might oblige me to a lengthened separation from you all and especially from my poor Louisa, but I could not refuse being in the council which is to assist the President till the 21st inst., when the votes of the people will have decided on the institutions proposed for its acceptation or rejection. That they will be accepted I have no doubt. My day was passed at the Ministère of the Intérieur from where I sent you news by telegraph. Leopold Le Hon [1] assisted me in this very obligingly.

The most disagreeable episode of the day was the meeting of about 200 deputies at the Mairie of the 10th Arrondissement, and there deciding on the *déchéance* of the President and the nomination of General Oudinot to command the parliamentary army—for which the only thing wanting was soldiers. They were taken between two files of soldiers from that place to the *Caserne* on the Quai d'Orsay, and I know from one of them, insulted by the people as they passed. I was very sorry that Broglie was among them. How-

[1] Son of Morny's friend the Comtesse Le Hon.

SOUTH EASTERN RAILWAY.

ELECTRIC TELEGRAPH.

London STATION.

At *11.10* A. M., on *Tuesday* the *2ⁿᵈ* day of *Dec* 185*1*.

RECEIVED the following Message :—

From	To
Name *M. de Morny*	Name *Countess Flahaut*
Address *Minister of the Interior*	Address *Grosvenor Square London.*

☞ **No Enquiry respecting this Message can be attended to without the production of this Paper.**

The Assembly is dissolved.
The President of the Republic
makes an appeal to the Country.

Signed *R.S. Rush*

TELEGRAM FROM MORNY TO MADAME DE FLAHAULT
December 2, 1851

ever, thank God he is in his own house. The rest comprising Barrot, Berryer, Piscatory, etc., etc., are either at Vincennes or the fort of the Mont Valérien. When at the *Caserne* of the Quai d'Orsay, Piscatory said to General Forey, "Vous faites-là un joli métier, Général," Forey replied, "Vous ferez bien, Monsieur, de ne pas faire l'insolent, parce que je vous ferai donner des coups de crosse."

You can have no idea of the enthusiastic spirit of the army. . . . All the reports of Paris and the departments are good. The name of Bonaparte and Napoleon act like magic. Madame de Lieven is in ecstasies of joy and so is Marion Ellice; I suppose her uncle pities little Thiers; nobody else does.

* Comte Walewski to Mme. de Flahault

[LONDON] *Wednesday midday* [*Dec. 3, 1851*].

Dear Madame de Flahault,

I have just received (10 o'clock) a telegraphic dispatch which left Paris at 9.30. "Paris and the departments are quiet." I have despatches from the Minister—still Turgot! [1] Morni [*sic*] has the ministry of the Interior; Fould the

---

[1] Walewski was apparently expecting Turgot to be replaced.

Treasury, Rouher justice and Magne [Public Works].

I have received all the proclamations; I have only one set of them, but if you happen to come to the embassy I will show them to you.

Everything is quiet and calm in Paris.

The President is to dine with the whole of the Corps diplomatique—including the minister of foreign affairs.

A thousand affectionate greetings.

A. W.

Here is a letter from M. de Flahault.

Flahault to Madame de Flahault

CABINET DU MINISTÈRE DE L'INTÉRIEUR,
Thursday, 3 o'clock [*December* 4, 1851]

The army is perfectly disposed and is in full march on the *émeute*. If, as I hope, it is well beaten everything will be over. You will have heard before you received this letter, for young Le Hon will send you a message.

Love to you all with all my heart.

Telegram

Received at 11 A.M. Thursday 4th December.

From: the Private Secretary of Minister of Interior, Paris.

PROCLAMATION
DU PRÉSIDENT DE LA RÉPUBLIQUE.

APPEL AU PEUPLE.

FRANÇAIS !

La situation actuelle ne peut durer plus longtemps. Chaque jour qui s'écoule aggrave les dangers du pays. L'Assemblée, qui devrait être le plus ferme appui de l'ordre, est devenue un foyer de complots. Le patriotisme de trois cents de ses membres n'a pu arrêter ses fatales tendances. Au lieu de faire les lois dans l'intérêt général, elle forge des armes pour la guerre civile; elle attente au pouvoir que je tiens directement du Peuple; elle encourage toutes les mauvaises passions; elle compromet le repos de la France; je l'ai dissoute, et je rends le Peuple entier juge entre elle et moi.

La Constitution, vous le savez, avait été faite dans le but d'affaiblir d'avance le pouvoir que vous alliez me confier. Six millions de suffrages furent une éclatante protestation contre elle, et cependant je l'ai fidèlement observée. Les provocations, les calomnies, les outrages m'ont trouvé impassible. Mais aujourd'hui que le pacte fondamental n'est plus respecté de ceux-là même qui l'invoquent sans cesse, et que les hommes qui ont déjà perdu deux monarchies veulent me lier les mains, afin de renverser la République, mon devoir est de déjouer leurs perfides projets, de maintenir la République, et de sauver le pays, en invoquant le jugement solennel du seul souverain que je reconnaisse en France, le Peuple.

Je fais donc un appel loyal à la nation tout entière, et je vous dis : Si vous voulez continuer cet état de malaise qui nous dégrade et compromet notre avenir, choisissez un autre à ma place, car je ne veux plus d'un pouvoir qui est impuissant à faire le bien, me rend responsable d'actes que je puis empêcher et m'enchaîne au gouvernail quand je vois le vaisseau courir vers l'abîme.

Si, au contraire, vous avez encore confiance en moi donnez-moi les moyens d'accomplir la grande mission que je tiens de vous.

Cette mission consiste à fermer l'ère des révolutions en satisfaisant les besoins légitimes du peuple et en le protégeant contre les passions subversives. Elle consiste surtout à créer des institutions qui survivent aux hommes et qui soient enfin des fondations sur lesquelles on puisse asseoir quelque chose de durable.

Persuadé que l'instabilité du Pouvoir, que la prépondérance d'une seule Assemblée sont des causes permanentes de trouble et de discorde, je soumets à vos suffrages les bases fondamentales suivantes d'une Constitution que les Assemblées développeront plus tard.

1° Un chef responsable nommé pour dix ans ;

2° Des ministres dépendant du pouvoir exécutif seul ;

3° Un conseil d'État formé des hommes les plus distingués préparant les lois et en soutenant la discussion devant le corps législatif ;

4° Un corps législatif discutant et votant les lois, nommé par le suffrage universel, sans scrutin de liste qui fausse l'élection ;

5° Une seconde Assemblée, formée de toutes les illustrations du pays, pouvoir pondérateur, gardien du pacte fondamental et des libertés publiques.

Ce système, créé par le Premier Consul au commencement du siècle, a déjà donné à la France le repos et la prospérité; il les lui garantirait encore.

Telle est ma conviction profonde. Si vous la partagez, déclarez-le par vos suffrages. Si, au contraire, vous préférez un gouvernement sans force, monarchique ou républicain, emprunté à je ne sais quel passé ou à quel avenir chimérique, répondez négativement.

Ainsi donc, pour la première fois depuis 1804, vous voterez en connaissance de cause, en sachant bien pour qui et pour quoi.

Si je n'obtiens pas la majorité de vos suffrages, alors je provoquerai la réunion d'une nouvelle Assemblée, et je lui remettrai le mandat que j'ai reçu de vous.

Mais si vous croyez que la cause dont mon nom est le symbole, c'est-à-dire la France régénérée par la Révolution de 89 et organisée par l'Empereur, est toujours la vôtre, proclamez-le en consacrant les pouvoirs que je vous demande.

Alors, la France et l'Europe seront préservées de l'anarchie, les obstacles s'aplaniront, les rivalités auront disparu, car tous respecteront, dans l'arrêt du peuple, le décret de la Providence.

Fait au palais de l'Élysée, le 2 décembre 1851.

LOUIS-NAPOLÉON BONAPARTE.

LE PRÉSIDENT DE LA RÉPUBLIQUE
DÉCRÈTE :

Art. 1.
L'Assemblée nationale est dissoute.

Art. 2.
Le suffrage universel est rétabli. La loi du 31 mai est abrogée.

Art. 3.
Le Peuple français est convoqué dans ses comices à partir du 14 décembre jusqu'au 21 décembre suivant.

Art. 4.
L'état de siège est décrété dans l'étendue de la 1re division militaire.

Art. 5.
Le Conseil d'État est dissous.

Art. 6.
Le Ministre de l'intérieur est chargé de l'exécution du présent décret.

Fait au Palais de l'Élysée, le 2 décembre 1851.

LOUIS-NAPOLÉON BONAPARTE.

Le Ministre de l'Intérieur,
DE MORNY.

PROCLAMATION
DU PRÉSIDENT DE LA RÉPUBLIQUE.
A L'ARMÉE.

SOLDATS !

Soyez fiers de votre mission, vous sauverez la Patrie, car je compte sur vous, non pour violer les lois, mais pour faire respecter la première loi du pays, la souveraineté nationale, dont je suis le légitime représentant.

Depuis longtemps vous souffrez comme moi des obstacles qui s'opposent et au bien que je voulais vous faire et aux démonstrations de votre sympathie en ma faveur. Ces obstacles sont brisés. L'Assemblée a essayé d'attenter à l'autorité que je tiens de la nation entière; elle a cessé d'exister.

Je fais un loyal appel au peuple et à l'armée, et je leur dis : ou donnez-moi les moyens d'assurer votre prospérité, ou choisissez un autre à ma place.

En 1830 comme en 1848, on vous a traités en vaincus. Après avoir flétri votre désintéressement héroïque, on a dédaigné de consulter vos sympathies et vos vœux, et cependant vous êtes l'élite de la Nation. Aujourd'hui, en ce moment solennel, je veux que l'armée fasse entendre sa voix.

Votre devoir librement consenti comme Citoyens, mais, comme soldats, n'oubliez pas que l'obéissance passive aux ordres du chef du Gouvernement est le devoir rigoureux de l'armée, depuis le général jusqu'au soldat. C'est à moi, responsable de mes actions devant le Peuple et devant la postérité, de prendre les mesures qui me semblent indispensables pour le bien public.

Quant à vous, restez inébranlables dans les règles de la discipline et de l'honneur. Aidez, par votre attitude imposante, le pays à manifester sa volonté dans le calme et la réflexion. Soyez prêts à réprimer toute tentative contre le libre exercice de la souveraineté du Peuple. Soldats, je ne vous parle pas des souvenirs que mon nom rappelle. Ils sont gravés dans vos cœurs. Nous sommes unis par des liens indissolubles. Votre histoire est la mienne. Il y a entre nous dans le passé communauté de gloire et de malheur. Il y aura dans l'avenir communauté de sentiments et de résolution pour le repos et la grandeur de la France.

Fait au Palais de l'Élysée, le 2 décembre 1851.

Signé LOUIS-NAPOLÉON BONAPARTE.

---

2 décembre. — 3 heures de l'après-midi.

La plus grande tranquillité règne dans Paris.

On annonce que MM. Changarnier, Cavaignac, Bedeau, Lamoricière, Le Flô et Charras, ont été arrêtés entre deux et trois heures, ainsi que quelques autres représentants. Tous ont été écroués à Vincennes.

M. de Morny a pris possession du ministère de l'intérieur. Il répond du maintien de la tranquillité dans Paris.

Le gérant : DENAIN.

PROCLAMATION OF THE COUP D'ÉTAT
Issued on the morning of December 2nd, 1851

THE COUP D'ÉTAT

To: the Countess Flahault, 19 Grosvenor Square.

Paris 9 o'clock is calm. The troubles of yesterday have been quickly and energetically repressed. The Minister of war has published a proclamation certifying that all individuals taken working at Barricades, or with arms in hands, would be immediately shot. This has spread terror amongst the rioters. The Departments are quiet. Nearly the whole of the Representatives of the 10th Arrondissement have been released.

Telegram

Received at 8.50 P.M. Thursday 4th December

4th December 7 o'clock. Insurrection put down. Troops gone to rest. Account of Departments excellent. No other town taken part in insurrection.

Signed (for the Minister) LEOPOLD LE BLANC.[1]

Flahault to Madame de Flahault

MINISTÈRE DE L'INTÉRIEUR,
December 5, 12 o'clock.[2]

Everything is going on well in Paris and better in the provinces where the enthusiasm is immense,

---

[1] Probably a mistake for Leopold Le Hon, who was now Morny's *chef de cabinet.*

[2] Postmark Dec. 5, 1851.

181

and most of the people cry "Vive Napoléon." Here the Legitimists are found mixed with the *Émeutiers*, and shots have been fired from houses of the Boulevard des Italiens, Rue Richelieu, etc. These houses have been broken in by the troops and good execution made. The soldiers are admirable.

The manner of voting, with the obligation to sign the register, was unpopular, and it has been changed to "tablet"[1] which has produced a very good effect. The *blouses* this morning were replacing the *pavés* and the women applauding the soldiers as they passed. Auguste is heroic and I wish all his colleagues were like him. We do all we can to prop them. I hope you have received the messages.

Telegram

Received at 7.2 P.M. Friday 5th December.

Minister of Foreign Affairs to Countess Flahault.

The insurrection is suppressed in all parts of Paris. The secret voting granted by yesterday's decree has produced the best effect. Accounts from all Departments are excellent. Tranquillity prevails everywhere and even enthusiasm.

[1] The original plan had been for an "open" vote, but this was now changed to a secret ballot.

THE COUP D'ÉTAT

Telegram

Received at 8.6 P.M. Friday 5th **December.**

From Auguste de Morny, Paris, to Madame Flahault.

All is over. We are victorious on all the line and all France approves. How glorious it would be to see the Society [1] preserved for a long period [*sic*].

Received at 4.55 P.M. Saturday 6th **December.**

From De Morny, to Madame de Flahault, London.

Greatest calm. Émeute vanquished and terrified [*sic*]. They are arresting the chiefs still at large. Intelligence from Departments continues to be excellent. *Rentes* at the present hour are 96 francs, 4 francs higher than yesterday.

Flahault to Emily Lady Shelburne

[PARIS] *Saturday* [*December 6th*].

You are quite right to have felt and still to feel alarm at what is going on. It was a tremendous game to play and which necessity alone could justify. When I determined on coming here, my

---

[1] The authors of the *coup d'état* were fond of justifying themselves as saviours of "La Société."

object was to try to bring about a reconciliation between the chiefs of the Majority and the President, so that the *coup d'état*, which everybody considered as indispensable and inevitable before 1852 (if the country was to be saved), should be the joint act of the Executive and Legislative Powers. I found most members of the Majority well disposed and the President authorised me to give his assent; but he added at the same time, that when it came to the point, I should find the chiefs I had seen and considered unwilling, incapable or powerless. Still I continued, but there came in succession the proposition of the *Questeurs* and the law on the responsibility of the President, in which the proposition of the *Questeurs* was to be again included.

All these measures were blamed by Broglie and his friends and yet they voted for them; and though the proposition of the *Questeurs* (for giving the Assembly the direct command of the troops) had been rejected,—owing to the unwillingness of the Montagne to give the President or Assembly that power, which it felt would be placing it in the hands of Changarnier,—yet it was known that an understanding had been come to by which Cavaignac was to be the General, which secured the votes of the Montagne and the adoption of what had at first been rejected. The result would have been civil war between a Presidential and Parliamentary army, the capital and country inundated with blood and the inevitable triumph of the *République démocratique* and *sociale*. It was known also that on the day that the proposition of the Questeurs was rejected, it had been adopted that the President should be *décrété d'accusation* and sent to Vincennes; and besides that there was a conspiracy in favour of the Prince de Joinville, which only wanted an opportunity *pour éclater*.

That is all bad enough, but what makes it worse is that it could only create confusion, anarchy and bloodshed, for the army cares for none of these African generals and feels enthusiasm for nothing but the name of Napoleon. Yet the danger was pressing, for the plots were ripe and might break out at any moment, and it was under these circumstances that a resolution was to be taken. Was the Assembly to be allowed to pursue its factious career till it had passed a vote destructive of the power of the President and then be expelled, with the danger of bloodshed, from the place of its sittings, or was it necessary to do what has been done? For my part I do not hesitate in approving the resolution

which has been taken and executed to the satis-
faction and joy of all the quiet and honest part of
the population, and I believe that all the friends
of their country who have more patriotism than
party spirit, are bound to stand by and support
the brave men who have risked their lives to
save their country.

For God's sake, my child, leave off judging
foreign events with English notions, which are
really not applicable to men or things here. . . .

Flahault to Madame de Flahault

[PARIS] *Dimanche [December 7]*.

I have received a letter from Emily written in
the disposition you mention and I have answered
it. Tell her to show you my answer. I certainly
mean to accept no office for in Louisa's [1] state
of health it would be the cause of too painful a
separation, but I cannot refuse Auguste and the
President the moral support they want, especially
at first. I hope to be with you on the 22nd or 23rd.

Many energetic measures must be taken and
it will be a great pity if the English Government
is short-sighted enough to judge of what passes
according to English principles and actions.

[1] Flahault's youngest daughter—she was consumptive and died
eighteen months later.

THE COUP D'ÉTAT

Everything is different—men and things. Read my letter to Emily, in which I have given her an account of the state of things which has led to the resolution taken and executed.[1] Every important person begins to admit that it was the only thing that could save the country from the dangers which threatens it, but Society will be intolerable this winter. Even families are so disunited that even at Passy [2] there is a complete separation. . . . Confidence is returning, the funds are rising, and the whole country except the *Society* [*sic*] rejoices at what has been done.

It is curious that Normandy should be so squeamish about what has taken place, he who took so easily and agreeably the violent destruction of Louis Ph[ilippe]'s government. . . . Adieu, my dearest Margaret, I long to be with you again, and as soon as the votes have been given you may depend on seeing me—the 23 or 24.

Postscript

Ma chère Louise,

J' ai recu et lu à Auguste votre aimable petit mot. Il en a été touché jusqu'au cœur. Pauvre garçon—il s'est admirablement conduit, mais il est l'objet de la haine de tous les représentans et de tout ce qui tient à eux. . . .

[1] See previous letter.   [2] *I.e.* amongst the Delesserts.

187

THE SECRET OF THE COUP D'ÉTAT

[PARIS] *Monday [December 8].*

I have very little time to-day, for Auguste and his friends take a great part of it and they have asked me to come to their meeting, where I have been uninterruptedly since that business began. However, you may depend that, unless forced by necessity, I shall do nothing that can separate us beyond the 22 or 23. . . . Everything is going on well, but Society is in the most acrimonious state—"*Ce n'est pas tenable.*" I wish there was no sea. I should have invited you and Georgina to have come and occupied Auguste's apartment. It would make him very happy and he has begged me to say so.

* Comte de Laubespin [1] *to Morny*

TRACY SUR LOIRE,
Monday, 8 December, 4 o'clock.

Well done, my dear friend, well done! Persevere with your enlightened dictatorship [2] and you will save France! Let this splendid phrase of the Prince's be your motto: "It is time that the wicked should tremble, and that good men should breathe again." As to my own family, my cousins are the only ones whose conduct I

[1] A rich landowner in Le Nièvre and an admirer of Morny's.
[2] *Dictature éclairée.*

can approve—Montalembert, Mérode and the rest
—stalwart champions of the cause of order. If
I was in Paris I would come to grasp your hand
and assure you that you have the sympathy of
all honest men. But I must stay in my own
unfortunate district, to keep in check the "Red"
agents (who are quaking in their impotence) and
to encourage those poor "moderates" who have
allowed themselves to be cruelly suppressed by
a reign of terror akin to that of 93. As far as I
can see, the anarchical movement has been suppressed in my Department. The military have
right well performed their part at Clancy, Neury,
etc. It is now for those in authority to show
such severity as is required.

My good wishes are with you.

LÉONEL DE LAUBESPIN.

Flahault to Madame de Flahault

[PARIS] *Wednesday* [10*th December*].

Why do you direct to the Ministère de l'Intérieur? I am still at the Champs Élysées and it
only makes me get your letters much later.

The first 3 days I passed almost entirely at
the *Intérieur* to assist Auguste and because he and
his colleagues asked me to assist at all their

deliberations, but since everything is quiet I only go there now and then. They wished [me] to come in, but I told them that that was impossible.

I should be in despair if your young friends [1] were as mad as you have been told, for they have no other chance than that of being taken. Every precaution has been made for shutting up every inlet. As for the little man,[2] he has consented to go abroad and went over the Rhine at Strasburg to-day.

There is no political agitation in any part of the territory, but a good many socialist and communist movements in several Departments— that is, châteaux and houses burnt and the proprietors killed. From all reports it appears that a general rise of that nature was to take place all over France, and the army would not have been sufficient to put it down. Everybody —even those who sulk—admits that the *coup d'état* has saved the country.

The President's intention is to make a constitution—that is to save a Senate, a Legislative Assembly and a Council of State. He is perfectly

[1] The Prince de Joinville and the Duc d'Aumale, who were making plans for a royalist insurrection in the north of France.

[2] Thiers. He was taken first to Mazas and then to Kehl on the Rhine, where on December 8 he was released. He then proceeded to Brussels, and in January to London.

quiet, and not at all elated with his success. On Monday his drawing-rooms were brim full, but none of the *représentans* or their families. Their arrestation was a *maladresse* on the part of the officer who did it, and who ought only to have dispersed them, but since then their imprisonment has been their own voluntary act.

Except with some very reasonable men, such as the Duc de Noailles and Broglie, and Montebello, the irritation is beyond all bounds. Nobody will meet. I was at Mme. de Lieven's yesterday with Montebello, who is one of the most moderate, and yet when Fould came in, he got up and went out without speaking or bowing. Poor Auguste has inspired hatreds that will never end. It is said that all the Deputies arrested are in a rage against Dupin, and I know for certain that Falloux told him that his conduct had been infamous. Poor, poor country! Every one of the Deputies who was preventively arrested at 6 in the morning, was in his own house, but everybody knows that it was a race between the Assembly and the President who should do the thing, and if he had delayed, he would have been arrested and put under accusation. I shall be very sorry if England is not pleased with what has been done, but all notions of a military despotism and warlike intentions are a perfect absurdity. The President is as friendly to England as his uncle was hostile.

The Orléans are not wise in conducting themselves as they do. By remaining quiet and expressing respect for any decision taken by France, they would have made their position better for any future eventuality. I am very sorry for them, but it is not possible to sacrifice the country to serve them without a chance even of doing them any good. If they commit any imprudence they will endanger their property.[1] . . . Every one cries out against my going.

[PARIS, *Saturday*] *December* 13.

For God's sake don't alarm yourself for such stuff as the anonymous letters you have received. Do you believe that there are many people ready to risk their life for the pleasure of revenge, and do you think that those scoundrels would draw lots to kill Auguste or me, while the President is alive? Feel no anxiety while I am here or in London, and be sure that I shall return there as safe from the Club as I do here. . . . Poor Emily, how her good judgment is carried away

---

[1] It may be observed that Flahault here shows an intelligent anticipation of the confiscation of the Orléans property, which actually took place by the decree of January 22, 1852 (*v. infra*).

THE COUP D'ÉTAT

by the nonsense and ignorance of the state of things of her friends.

[PARIS] *Sunday* [*December* 14].

Everything is going on as well as one could wish except in some Departments of the South, where Socialism (denied by your friends at Panshanger [1]) asserts itself by murder, plunder, fire and cruelties and brutalities which respect neither age nor sex. There is hardly any one in this country, except those in whom party spirit extinguishes all other feeling, who does not admit that in 1852, what now takes place in some localities, would have covered the whole country and been too powerful for the army to have suppressed it. From all the Departments come thanksgiving and blessings to those who have had the courage to save the country from such misfortunes. I could quote to you authorities which are entitled to a little more respect on those matters than those who know nothing of the state of the country and judge of everything on the principle of "King, Lords and Commons."

[1] We learn from Henry Greville, who was one of the party then staying at Panshanger with Lord and Lady Cowper, that it consisted of the Cannings, Sydneys, Bessboroughs, Shelburnes, De Mauley, Granville, F. Leveson, and Charles Greville—besides Mme. de Flahault and her unmarried daughter Georgine.

Dumond is arrived from his Department in the South, and though from a feeling of propriety and attachment to his friends he does not adhere to the Government, admits that by his *coup d'état* the President has saved the country. He says that even in Paris no one can have a notion how low the Assembly had fallen in public opinion. I could quote to you Pasquier, Ségur (the father not the son, who cuts me dead), Guizot, most of the Legitimists, the Duc de Noailles, etc., etc., etc. I don't mention Montalembert, Mérode, and all impartial men. The only ones who are violent are the Orleanists, who had hoped to make the *coup d'état* against the President. Every proof has been found of this in M. Baze's [1] papers, and if those of the other persons arrested had been seized, it would have shown that they were all in the plot. But that formality was neglected, and even those of M. Baze were only thought of five days after his arrestation. What is very amusing is that there is a great outcry against the Government for having arrested Deputies who were assembled to decree the *déchéance* of the President, to forbid all authorities civil and military obeying him, who had named a General

---

[1] One of the three *questeurs de la chambre* who were arrested in the small hours of December 2.

194

to take command of the troops, and were actually proclaiming their decree from the window to the people by the mouth of Berryer! In old times of civil war they would have been shot, and they are furious against me because I say that they only showed this Roman dignity and energy because they knew there was no danger.

I was in hopes that I could have voted to-day in which case I should have set out to-morrow, but I cannot do it till next Sunday. God grant that the President may have 7 millions of votes. If they had any sense at Claremont they would have told all their adherents to vote for him, and it would have done more for their future chances than anything they can do.

Persigny to Flahault

PARIS, 14 *December* 1851.

Monsieur le Comte,

I am commanded by the Prince President to say that he wishes to include your name in the Commission on the Constitution.[1] He invites you to come to the Élysée to-morrow, Monday, at 10 o'clock in the morning.

---

[1] The *commission consultative* which was set up pending the formation of the *conseil d'état*. Victor Hugo gives a list of its members (*Histoire d'un crime*).

THE SECRET OF THE COUP D'ÉTAT

Pray accept the assurance of my highest esteem and devotion. F. DE PERSIGNY

Russell to Lansdowne

The letter which follows, though not especially concerned with the French *coup d'état*, relates to its principal "bye-product" in England—the dismissal of Lord Palmerston. Further documents on the same subject will be found in their order of date (Lansdowne to Russell, Dec. 18; Russell to Lansdowne, Dec. 18; Lansdowne to Russell, Dec. 21 and 23; Lansdowne to Palmerston, Dec. 24; Clarendon to Lansdowne, Dec. 25; and Palmerston to Lansdowne, Dec. 29).

Lord Normanby, the British Ambassador in Paris, had for some time before the *coup d'état* shown marked sympathy with the "Burgraves" or party of the Assembly, and was notoriously hostile to Louis Napoleon. Palmerston on the other hand was inclined to view the President's actions with a friendly eye, and had expressed his sympathies to Walewski, the French Ambassador, the day after the *coup d'état* took place (December 3). Palmerston's approval was privately communicated by Walewski to Turgot, the French Foreign Minister, who in his turn had spoken to Normanby of the British minister's attitude.

196

THE COUP D'ÉTAT

Normanby complained to John Russell, and on December 19 the Prime Minister dismissed his Foreign Secretary, who two days later was replaced by Lord Granville.

It was not till some time afterwards that the inner history of this transaction transpired. It is contained in a letter amongst the Lansdowne papers, written by Palmerston to Lansdowne on October 4, 1852, and first published in 1876. From this it appears that Russell had himself expressed to Walewski on two occasions (December 4 and 6)—in terms if anything stronger than those for which he now attacked Palmerston—his own approval of the *coup d'état*, and that it was only after receiving this assurance from the Prime Minister that Walewski had made any official communication to the French Government. It is thus clear that the alleged ground for the dismissal was merely a pretext and this inference is strengthened by what afterwards occurred.

The matter was to come up for discussion at the opening of Parliament on Feb. 3, and Russell had meanwhile become aware that his conversations with Walewski of December 4 and 6 were known to Palmerston. Russell was therefore compelled to shift his ground, and when the debate took place he justified his action on the score that Palmerston had contravened the directions for the general conduct of foreign affairs which had been laid down in a memorandum by Queen Victoria more than a year before the *coup d'état* took place (August 1850).

Palmerston was somewhat taken aback by this change of front, and from motives entirely creditable to him was unwilling to embark on a discussion in which he would seem to have been pitted against his Sovereign. He therefore made a somewhat lame defence, and the Prime Minister was generally considered to have carried off the honours of the debate. The ex-Foreign Secretary had, however, not long to wait for his revenge. On February 20 he proposed and carried against the Government an amendment to the Militia Bill. Russell was forced to resign and Lord Derby assumed the conduct of affairs.

The episode is recounted in detail in Evelyn Ashley's *Life of Viscount Palmerston*, in which all the documents are printed *in extenso*.

WOBURN ABBEY, *Dec.* 15, 1851.

I have very unpleasant letters from Normanby. It appears that Palmerston has remonstrated with him on his hostility to the President [1]—latterly

[1] Cf. Palmerston's letters to Normanby of December 3 and 5, quoted in Ashley's *Life of Palmerston*, pp. 289 and 292.

in very disagreeable terms, and saying the President might, he was afraid, ask for his recall.

I am determined to support Normanby in this matter. He was right to tell us what he believed to be the truth, though it might not agree with our opinions. But what is still graver is that Normanby writes in a dispatch,[1] that Turgot told him that his official resumption of diplomatic relations was of less consequence, as Palmerston had told Walewski that he entirely approved of what had been done and that the President could not do otherwise.

This is so contrary to the line of neutrality in the intimate affairs of France, prescribed by the Queen, and adopted by Palmerston, that the Queen is justly offended at it.

I cannot stand any more of these *tracasseries,* but I hope to have some explanation from Palmerston to-morrow.

Flahault to Madame de Flahault

[PARIS] *Wednesday* 17 [*December*].

I cannot send you the pamphlet you wish, for it was the only copy I had and it is not for sale. . . . Keep this for yourself, but this commission

[1] December 6.

I told you I was of, which is very select, is for carrying out what is treated in it. What I mentioned to you has been pressed upon me,[1] but I cannot leave my poor Louise permanently, as that would make it necessary.

Auguste shows activity, ability and firmness above all praise. Notwithstanding the pressure of business, he remodels his administrations, diminishes the number of employés, increases the salary of those retained—in short, shows a master mind. His orders for clearing Paris and France of those scoundrels who have caused all the revolutions and disasters are firm, and for the first time, instead of being called *des hommes égarés*, they are branded with their deserved designation of *bandits* and *coquins*. I send you the two last that have appeared.

The appearance of the country is completely changed. Honest men are looking up and all the demagogues are terrified. Funds are rising and affairs improving all over the country. . . . The papers do not mention the tenth part of the atrocities committed by the insurgents. Schools [2] of young girls violated, women killed after horrid

[1] Probably the command of the *garde nationale*, which, it appears from a later letter (January 23), had been offered to Flahault about this time.

[2] A convent had been broken into in Nivernais.

tortures—in short, they are cannibals corrupted by civilization. This country must be regenerated by an energetic government, for since Napoleon it has been demoralized by weakness.

I daresay that Thiers will turn more and more the heads of the poor people at C.[1] and make them take a hostile part against the President, while their interest would be to ally themselves to the popular feeling and rejoice that the country has been saved. They should not forget that they have here 8 millions sterling of property and that people are not wanting who advise its sequestration.[2]

Lansdowne to Russell

BOWOOD, Dec. 18 [1851].

All party arrangements, tho' it is necessary to attend to them, appear infinitely small, when compared with the great stakes that are now being played for in the world at large; for I have no idea that the present state of things can continue in France without affecting more or less all other countries. I quite agree with you that

[1] Claremont.
[2] It would have been interesting if Flahault had informed us who were the "people" who were then suggesting the confiscation of the Orléans property. The proposal is generally supposed to have emanated from Persigny.

strict neutrality, avoiding the example of Austria and Prussia, is the ground we ought to occupy as long as we possibly can, and do hope that neither Palmerston on the one hand, nor Normanby on the other, have in any degree departed from it. It is certainly supposed at Paris, that Normanby latterly has shown a leaning against the President.

I suspect that Walewski, without any bad intention, is not entirely to be depended upon for accuracy, in reports he may make of conversations.

Russell to Lansdowne

WOBURN ABBEY, *Dec.* 18, 1851.

My dear Lord Lansdowne,

Things have come to such a pass with Palmerston, that it is impossible we can go on together, while he holds the Foreign Office.

It appears that on Dec. 3 he expressed to Walewski some approbation of the *coup d'état* of Louis Napoleon, which was quoted at Paris by Turgot as the approbation of the British Government.

When the Queen asked through me for an explanation of this strange circumstance (which seemed so contrary to our professions of not interfering in the internal affairs of France),

Palmerston at first did not answer, but wrote a dispatch to Normanby,[1] and sent it unseen by the Queen, or by me, affirming his own opinions in favour of the measure of the 2nd Dec.

This conduct appeared to me so wanting in propriety, so wanting in respect to the Queen, that we could not go on any longer.

While in this mood, I received a long letter from Palmerston, entirely in justification of Louis Napoleon.[2]

I answered that he had mistaken the question; that it was not whether Louis Napoleon was right or wrong, but whether *he* was justified as the Queen's Sectry. of State in giving an opinion which had not been given by the Cabinet, and which is in contradiction to that abstinence from all interference prescribed to Lord Normanby. I therefore said that I did not think he could remain Foreign Secretary with advantage to the country, but that if he would accept the office of Lord Lieutenant of Ireland, I was sure Clarendon would willingly give it up to him,[3] without

---

[1] *I.e.* Palmerston's dispatch to Normanby of December 16, quoted in Ashley's *Life of Lord Palmerston*, p. 297.

[2] *I.e.* Palmerston's letter of December 16 to John Russell, quoted in Ashley's *Life of Lord Palmerston*, p. 300.

[3] But the proposal was never made to Clarendon, since Palmerston refused to consider the tentative offer.

looking to any other office. There the matter rests at present. On Saturday, if I hear nothing further, I shall lay these letters before the Queen.

You will agree with me in thinking this a very painful matter. We have often contemplated this termination together and never without embarrassment. At the present moment it appears to me no one would be so fit a successor as Ld. Granville. He is liberal, firm, conciliatory, and a good speaker in Parliament.

I have summoned the Cabinet for Monday, when I shall go up to town. In the meantime, I shall be glad to hear from you. Yrs. truly,

J. RUSSELL.

Flahault to Madame de Flahault

[PARIS] *Thursday* 18 [*December*].

We have had some of the pamphlets you wish to have printed, and I send you to-day 10 by the Embassy. Enclosed I send you an extract of a newspaper in which a pretended letter of General Cavaignac had been inserted, in which he was made to say of the President: "He is more powerful than his uncle, you must come over to his side." It was this that induced Auguste to write to the *rédacteur*.

THE COUP D'ÉTAT

Mme. Odier[1] wrote to Auguste some days ago to obtain an order of admission to the prison in which she wished the marriage of her daughter to be performed. He wrote the following answer[2]:

"Madam,

"The President of the Republic has been forced to take in the first instance some strong measures in which all personal considerations have of necessity been disregarded, but he has expressed to me the wish that as soon as order is re-established General Cavaignac should be set at liberty. He has not forgotten the good services which have been rendered by him to Society in the cause of law and order, and he is far from placing him in the same category as the conspirators who thought to destroy his authority.

Being well aware of the views held by all the members of your family, and at the same time desirous of giving them a proof of his friendly disposition, he has ordered me to tell you that he would be grieved to think that the marriage ceremony between your daughter and the honourable General should take place in the melancholy surroundings of a prison, and to send you the

[1] Sister of Laborde and, according to Viel-Castel, Thiers's mistress.
[2] Translated.

order of his release. I need hardly tell you how pleased I am to carry out these instructions, and I beg you to accept the assurance of my deep respect.   MORNY."

I hope you like it—Hand it to our friends. [1]

[PARIS] *Friday* 19 [*December*].

The Legitimists and Orleanists try to deny, or treat lightly, the horrors committed in the provinces, but all those on the spot or who return from thence, speak too loud and feelingly on the subject for the truth not to prevail. I am very anxious to get to Bowood, but *our work* is very difficult—one progresses but slowly.

I don't "poo-poo" your fears, my dear Margaret, and I am grateful for them; only I am convinced that the scoundrels whose threats cause them, are a set of cowards, whose courage is only caused by those who fear them. Auguste's proclamations is the only way to deal with them [*sic*].

I wish very much that people in England would take a more reasonable and correct view of the state of things here. The gratitude of all the honest men in the country, whose opinion is

[1] Morny was evidently pleased with this composition. He gave a copy also to Dr. Véron, who printed it in his *Mémoires d'un bourgeois de Paris*.

not biassed by party spirit, ought to open their eyes. . . .

You ask me some questions about Society. The state of irritation is beyond anything you can imagine. Old friends pass by one another in the street, without giving a sign of recognition, and the arrival of one disagreeable face will put a whole salon to flight. Poor Mme. de Lieven remained quite alone some nights, each party being afraid of meeting the other. Canouville was near passing me in the street without stopping, but I took him by the collar and had some conversation; but he is *très monté*. La Redorte is perfectly mad, and furious at not being arrested: his wife[1] and the Maréchale are, I hear, moderate, but I have not seen them. Except my old *camarade* the General, the Ségurs are *inabordable*, Amélie a perfect fury. The *Club de l'Union* as hostile as possible. The *Jockey* more presidential. I hear that some of those who have been arrested and since liberated are pretty reasonable—Roger, Piscatory, Lasteyrie, Rémusat—but their wives are perfect furies. The Generals at Ham are not violent except Bedeau, who *I say* is in a rage

[1] She was the daughter of Marshal d'Albuféra.

207

because he has seen done what he had the cowardice not to do in 1848.

I sent you Auguste's letter to Mme. Odier, it was a good and kind one. Judge of his astonishment on receiving (Thursday) the following letter [1] from Cavaignac:

"FORT DE HAM, 17 *Dec.* 1851.

"Monsieur le Ministre,

"Mme. Odier, who is soon to become my mother-in-law, has this moment handed to me the order for my release. With this order there is a letter which you have addressed to her. If the commandant of the Fort de Ham, had without more ado been ordered to open to me the gates of this prison, I should (also without more ado) have resumed the liberty of which I have been illegally deprived. But the necessary order is accompanied by a letter which you surely did not intend to be treated as confidential and which was very naturally communicated to me. The comments contained in it and the motives which it assigned to the person in whose name you are acting, are not of a kind which I can accept.

"It is quite true that no one could regret more acutely than I do, that I should enter upon my

[1] Translated.

union with Mademoiselle Odier under such sad circumstances, but I will not admit, nor indeed will she, that such considerations should be the reason for my restoration to freedom. I am entitled, M. le Ministre, to leave this place for one reason only,—and that is that I have done nothing which can justify my detention here. It is not my duty to remain a prisoner against the wishes of those who have illegally detained me, but I do regard it as my duty and as a point of honour, not to accept tacitly the compromise which has been suggested.

"Consequently, M. le Ministre, I have the honour to inform you that I shall remain here till Friday evening the 19th of this month; I shall then hand to the Commandant of the Fort the order, which I am keeping by me. If he has by that time received no instructions to the contrary, I shall hold myself free to say, and to take it as accepted by the Government, that (as I have stated above) I leave my prison for the sole reason that there was no just cause for keeping me there.

CAVAIGNAC."

Remark the contrast between the language and the act. The letter is written on the 17th, received on the 18th, and answered on the 19th —the day fixed for his leaving the prison.

This is that answer:

"General,

"When I sent Madame Odier the order for your release, I had no other object in view than that of doing a kindness to a family which I love and respect. I never dreamt of anything else. If I allowed myself to mention the personal feelings of the President of the Republic, it was because —as you know better than any one—though great political movements undertaken for the country's good sometimes necessitate hard measures, these need not impair the high opinion one may both feel and express for one's adversaries.

"Please therefore do not misunderstand me if I do not reply to what you have done me the honour to say as to the illegality of your arrest. I will merely congratulate you that the 19th— the date you have yourself selected—is not far distant.   MORNY."

Very good, is it not?

Mme. de Girardin is all kindness to me. Her hatred is for Claremont, and even if the Comte de Chambord were dead, she would prefer infinitely the President to the Comte de Paris. Girardin is vehemently presidential.

Mme. de Lobau is violent against the President and what has been done . . . all reports from the Departments on the Elections promise well.

21 [*December*].

I voted yesterday, and from what the Mayor told me the elections seem to be favourable. The *ouvriers* are well disposed. Adieu: I must leave off to dress and go to the Élysée where we have a meeting.

Flahault returned to England on December 25, and as subsequent letters show, rejoined his family on December 27 or 28 at Bowood, where he remained for a week.

Lansdowne to Russell

THE GRANGE,
Sunday morning [21 *December* 1851].

My dear J. Russell,

I have only this moment received your very painful communication [1] and, as the post here goes out at twelve, have but little time to write. I shall, however, at whatever inconvenience, go to town to-morrow early before I return to Bowood.

---

[1] Of December 18 (*supra*), for, as Lansdowne explains to Palmerston on December 24, this letter had gone astray, owing to his absence from Bowood.

I shall call therefore in Downing Street before two in hopes of seeing you, and glad indeed I shall be to hear this sad affair has been brought —if indeed it is possible to bring it—to any satisfactory conclusion.

Palmerston's line, as stated, appears to me quite inexplicable. I cannot believe that there is one member of the Cabinet, including himself, who would state that as a Government (and he is the foreign organ of the Government) we ought to give an opinion as to what has passed in France; and he must have acted as he has done, which is very possible, on the belief (common at Paris) that Normanby had expressed opinions in the opposite direction, and that it was necessary to correct any misapprehension which might arise from it. But this he might have explained to you and to the Queen.

This will prove, if there is a positive disruption in the Govt., so great an increase of difficulty in the prospects of the session, that I should doubt the possibility of your carrying through any important measure. But as I shall see you so soon, I say nothing more.—Yours ever truly,

LANSDOWNE.

Grey is here and goes up also.

THE COUP D'ÉTAT

Lansdowne to Russell

BOWOOD, *Dec. 23rd* [1851].

My dear J. Russell,

Ever since we separated yesterday I have been
thinking with great anxiety of the bad effect on
the character and interests both of the Govt.
and the country which may be produced by
the reports consequent on the event of yesterday,
as soon as it is generally known (and by this time
I conclude it must be) and which will not fail to
be misrepresented and distorted by the whole
diplomacy of Europe, into a change, not in the
conduct but in the principles of our foreign policy.
Were Parlt. sitting this would easily be set to
rights, but a great deal of mischief may be done,
and I trust you may find some means of giving
it an authentic contradiction. The *Globe* newspaper, which has frequently done harm to the
Govt. by its apparently inserted articles, might
at least in this case be made to do some
good.

Having experienced the embarrassment of de-
laying such arrangements too late and finding
that Albemarle was just setting out for Nice, I
proposed to him if he could return for the meeting
of Parlt. to move the address, which he will. I

did this concluding you wished me to continue to act in all such matters as if I had "a life in the lease." I thought of Lord Meath for a seconder.—Yours ever, LANSDOWNE.

Lansdowne to Palmerston [1]

BOWOOD, *December 24.*

My dear Palmerston,

I cannot resist the desire I feel to write to you, and give some expression to the deep concern I feel at the event which has just occurred, of the probability of which I was only made aware the day before the last Cabinet, by two letters from J. Russell, which, owing to the accident of my being absent from home, reached me at the same time, when there appeared to be no room left for further and more satisfactory explanation.

I have felt this concern the more deeply because I am perfectly convinced there was and is no difference in the Cabinet with respect to the neutral position to be maintained in French affairs, and because I have felt inclined from the first to the same individual opinion (the grounds of which you stated in your letter to J. Russell)

[1] Printed in Ashley's *Life of Lord Palmerston.*

214

as to the necessity of a *coup d'état* by one person
to give France any chance of a peaceable future;
though I wish such opinions had not been expressed to an ambassador, apparently not very
well disposed to receive them, without having
been previously communicated to J. Russell and
to the Queen, knowing as I long have known the
extent of susceptibility which prevailed in that
quarter on these matters. This I have both
greatly lamented, and unsuccessfully laboured to
combat.

What I chiefly wish, however, to say to you
on this occasion is, that not only have I approved
of every essential act during your administration
of foreign affairs at the time, but that there is
not one with respect to which upon subsequent
reflection I could wish to recall my approbation.
Your policy will never, while you live, want the
ablest of all defenders, but whether in or out of
office (and J. Russell is well apprised upon what
a slender thread my own tenure of office now
hangs), I can never hear it impugned in public or
in private without expressing my conviction and
admiration of its great ability, and real consistency with the interests, and above all, the
honour of the country.—Yours sincerely,

LANSDOWNE.

THE SECRET OF THE COUP D'ÉTAT

Clarendon to Lansdowne

VICEREGAL LODGE, *Xmas Day* [1851].

My dear Lansdowne,

The event [1] took me by surprise because, as so many things of the same kind had been borne for so long, I saw no reason for an exception to what seemed a general rule. I am glad, however, it has been made, for as troublous times may be oncoming, it is desirable not to have *all* the Powers of Europe hostile to us and panting for our humiliation.

I am sure that Granville's appointment is the best that under the circumstances could have been made. He will do the business very well and be amenable to Lord John and agreeable to the Queen and the Corps Diplomatique.

I did not decline the F.O. as in fact it was not offered to me, and I only learnt the wish of the Cabinet that I should take it, by the same letter that announced Granville's acceptance. On Saturday last [2] Lord J. wrote me an account of what had passed with Palmerston and saying that though Lewis inclined to Granville, knowing my objections to succeed P., yet that the Cabinet might think otherwise and I must be prepared

[1] *I.e.* Palmerston's dismissal.　　　　[2] December 20.

for my fate. I stated frankly in a letter which
reached him on *Tuesday* what I thought were the
objections to myself: viz. that P.'s absurd jealousy and suspicions of me would induce him
to think I was the author of his downfall, and to
revenge it, he and his friends would get up an
opposition that would impair any power of use-
fulness I might possess, and 2ndly, that I should
not be agreeable to the Queen. But having said
so much I placed myself in his hands for whatever
he thought best, only requesting that he would
inform the Cabinet (and if possible Palmerston)
that I knew nothing about the causes of disagreement and accepted the F.O. reluctantly.

Ld. J. on Monday ¹ made his report to the
Queen and found in her and the Prince so strong
an objection to me (as I well knew there would
be) that on his return from Windsor he wrote to
me: "I tell you fairly that what would give me
most ease would be that you should waive the
office for yourself and acquiesce in the appointment of Granville." Shortly afterwards he received the letter from me I have alluded to above,
which he said relieved him from any difficulties,
and he at once sent for Granville.

I have troubled you with these details because

¹ December 22.

THE SECRET OF THE COUP D'ÉTAT

I have a presentiment that if any complaint is made about my not having been preferred to G. (as being more experienced—or any other ground that party spirit may select) it will be said that I absolutely refused and left Lord J. no option at a moment of embarrassment when my services were required. If such should be the case I cannot allow it to pass uncontradicted, for altho' I am perfectly satisfied with the arrangement made, yet I was prepared to waive my own personal objections *if* the cabinet had wished it and *if* the Queen had not been adverse. The latter consideration would of course under any circumstances have been conclusive, as nothing could have induced me to thrust myself upon her or to encounter the *guerre sourde* which has been waged so long from Windsor against the F.O. If my presentiment is unfounded, so much the better; if not I must rely upon your friendship to guard me against misconception. [1]

I am glad to find Lord J. means to reinforce the Government if he can. It is very necessary

[1] Russell's conduct towards Clarendon appears to have been somewhat disingenuous in this matter, and the impression is corroborated by Russell's letter to Lansdowne of December 18 (*supra*). This shows that the Prime Minister had from the first intended Granville (and not Clarendon) as Palmerston's successor, though it seems that when his colleagues expressed a contrary view, Russell allowed it to be supposed that he had definitely offered the post to Clarendon.

and will be all the more so if P. goes into active opposition. He proposes *inter alia* that the D. of Newcastle should come here and that I should go to Paris. The former would be an excellent arrangement, the latter a very unnecessary one.

After the first 8 and 40 hours I never doubted the success of the *coup d'état* or that the Prince's audacity would command respect and support. By way of a phase in their history, the French will be just as well pleased with a military despotism as a sham Republic, and it's nonsense to measure their loss of constitutional liberty by our standard. Louis Napoleon is evidently copying his uncle in all things great and small, and I expect the time will come when the invasion of England will be thought the most effectual means of consolidating his usurpation. I should like to know Flahault's opinion upon this. Ever yours truly,   CLARENDON

* Report from de Maupas to Louis Napoleon

In his recently published work, *Louis Napoleon and the Recovery of France*, Mr. F. A. Simpson points out that the heaviest charge against Napoleon III and the authors of the *coup d'état* lies in the massacre of inoffensive citizens which took place in Paris on December 4, 1851, and that the measure

219

of their condemnation must depend in some degree on the extent of the death-roll. Mr. Simpson (p. 172 foll.) proceeds to examine the various estimates, which have been made both at the time and since, of the casualties on that occasion. Lord Normanby, the British Ambassador, in a despatch of December 9, assured his Government that more than 2000 people exclusive of the military had been killed; the Comte de Viel Castel gave a similar figure in his *Memoirs* published in 1881, while the *Times* in an article of August 28, 1852, made the total something over 1200 in killed and wounded. After reviewing the evidence, Mr. Simpson inclines to the latter figure, and emphasises the obvious interest which the President and his friends had in minimising it, as well as the fact that no official document exists in the Archives of the Tuileries to disprove these estimates.

The report which follows seems to provide the necessary refutation. It is the original of the second report—the first had been sent in on December 15 —made by Maupas, the Prefect of Police, to the President on the matter at issue, and its absence from the official records is explained by the fact that it was sent (*infra*, p. 239) to Flahault in London, in order that he might contradict the exaggerated reports in the place whence they for the most part emanated, and that it has ever since remained hidden amongst the papers in the possession of his descendants. It would seem, from Flahault's letters, that the prejudice in high places was so strong that he found difficulty in making use of the document. The *Times* refused to print it, and it appeared in the *Morning Post* as given below, both unconvincing in form and extremely inaccurate in detail.

The document bears the impress of truth, for it is hard to believe that Maupas in reporting direct to the President could have deliberately manufactured his figures for the purposes of propaganda. His first report (*Memoires sur le Second Empire*, p. 509) gave, exclusive of the military, a total of 183 killed and 115 wounded, or 298 in all. The second, issued on Dec. 25, gives 215 killed and 119 wounded, a total of 334. The increment in the figures, after ten days' additional inquiry, is such as might be expected if they had been honestly compiled in both instances. An additional total of 210 (26 killed and 184 wounded) must be added for the military casualties, and we thus reach a grand total of all casualties, both civil and military, of 241 killed and 303 wounded, or 544 in all. The official figure, generally given as 600, would therefore have been one which would have allowed an ample margin for casualties undiscovered.

In November, 1851, it was generally agreed that France could not hope to emerge from the anomalous position in which her Government had been placed as a result of the second revolution, without further trouble and bloodshed. Apologists for the *coup d'état* might perhaps claim that, as things were, the "butcher's bill" was not an unduly large one. It secured at any rate for their country a long period of internal peace and prosperity, during which she occupied almost the foremost place in Europe.

OFFICE OF THE PREFECT OF POLICE,
PARIS, 25 *December* 1851.

REPORT

I have this moment received the information which the Prince has done me the honour to require, as to the number of insurgents who were killed and wounded in the course of the recent occurrences. I have not yet got the figures which I have asked for from the Ministry for war—these when received will complete my task.

Excluding therefore the military, the number of dead is approximately 215, of whom 137 were killed at the barricades, and 88 died from their wounds, or were accidentally killed, having taken no part in the rising. The number of these regrettable incidents is about 8 to 10.

The number of wounded is upwards of 119, without reckoning cases which may have been concealed from us from fear of ulterior consequences.

I shall now proceed, on the basis of these figures, to make the report on the matter as a whole which the Prince has done me honour to demand.

Paris hails with joy the outcome of the great events which have just taken place. Public opinion is increasingly in favour of the repression of disorder, and of the strongest possible organisation for this purpose.

The Prefect of Police,

DE MAUPAS.

The "Morning Post" version of De Maupas' report (published, as "from our Paris Correspondent," January 5, 1852)

The statistical return prepared by the Minister of War has not yet supplied the exact number of soldiers killed during the recent events in Paris.

Exclusive of casualties among the troops, the amount killed is 315, of whom 187 fell in the barricades and 88 died of wounds, or were killed accidentally without having taken part in the émeute. The number of the latter class, whose fate is much to be regretted, is 8 or 10.

The number of wounded is 115 without reckoning those whom a fear of ultimate consequences may have induced to conceal themselves from our researches.

* Morny to Flahault

FROM THE ELYSÉE,
26 December 1851.

My dear friend,

The Prince wishes to depute you to communicate officially to the English Government the result of the Election.

You will receive a formal appointment for this purpose, and I have accepted on your behalf.

I embrace you and all the family. In haste,

AUGUSTE.

We are nearing 7,000,000 votes.[1]

* Flahault to Morny

[LONDON, 27 December 1851.]

My dear friend,

I have received your letter and lose no time in replying to it. I told the Prince that he might

---

[1] The final result of the vote which ratified the *coup d'état* was nearly 7,500,000 for and 640,000 against. The figures were declared about December 30.

Cabinet
99
PRÉFET DE POLICE.

Paris le 29 X^{bre} 1851.

Rapport

Je reçois à l'instant le résultat de l'enquête que m'a fait l'honneur de m'ordonner le Prince, sur le nombre des insurgés morts ou blessés pendant les derniers événements. Je n'ai point encore la statistique du ministère de la Guerre, que j'ai réclamée et qui complettera mon travail. En dehors donc de la troupe, le nombre des morts est de 215, dont 187 tués sur les barricades et 28 morts des suites de leurs blessures, ou tués accidentellement sans avoir pris part à l'émeute. Le nombre de ces regrettables accidents est de 8 à 10 environ.

Le nombre des blessés est de 119, sans compter ceux que la crainte des poursuites a pu soustraire à nos recherches.

Je vais, maintenant, que j'en ai les bases, m'occuper de faire sur l'ensemble des événements le rapport que m'a fait l'honneur de me demander le Prince.

Paris jouit d'un calme parfait, et commence à devenir curieux de savoir quelles seront les conséquences des grands événements qui viennent de s'accomplir. L'opinion publique se prononce de plus en plus, pour le régime de répression le plus fortement organisé possible.

Le Préfet de Police,

de Maupas

DE MAUPAS' REPORT
ON THE CASUALTIES OF THE COUP D'ÉTAT

count on me for any service which I could render, and you know how anxious I am to keep that promise. He can therefore rely on my zeal and devotion, but I do not feel sure that if I were in his place I should give to the announcement which he wishes to delegate to me, the importance of a special mission. In dealing with crowned heads, with all their formalities and customs, one must be prepared to meet with difficulties, and the announcement might not be received in a manner befitting its importance.

There is no precedent to follow except that of the United States, and I do not think the President there has ever notified his election in this way. You will remember that I gave this as my opinion, with regard of all foreign courts, when I was in Paris. All such communications would in these days be best made through the regular diplomatic channel.

Flahault to Morny

BOWOOD, 28 *December* [1851].

My dear friend,

I saw yesterday morning Lord John Russell and Lord Granville and had a long conversation with each of them.

227

THE SECRET OF THE COUP D'ÉTAT

There is no doubt that Palmerston's dismissal, for this is what it amounts to, was due to Turgot's having communicated to Normanby the contents of the despatches and confidential letters which he had received from Walewski. There could not be much use in making such a communication, for there was nothing to be gained by informing Normanby of the attitude of his own government —the inevitable result of doing so was to cause annoyance, since he had himself received no direct instructions. It is quite natural that he should have complained. When Lord John Russell discovered what Palmerston had told Walewski, he was much hurt to find that the Minister of foreign affairs had, without asking his authority, spoken in the name of Her Majesty's government. The minister had often before acted in a similar manner, there had been quarrels in the cabinet and considerable ill feeling; so—on the principle that it is the last drop of water which makes the cup overflow—this fresh indiscretion sealed his fate.

Must we then conclude that the English government is moved by ill will towards the President or towards France? I think I can assure you that such is not the case. I do not mean to say by this that the nature of the *coup d'état,* the interference with personal liberty which it involved, the suppression of the national representatives, and the suspension of the liberty of the press, are not all measures antipathetic to the ideas, to the principles and to the prejudices of the English. But from all that I have heard said, as well as from general observation, I have no hesitation in asserting that the English Government (while anxious to make no definite pronouncement on recent events) has every intention of maintaining the most amicable relations, and that it is keenly desirous that the President should bring his undertaking to a triumphant conclusion.

This is the whole story, and the reason of the ministerial adjustment which has just taken place, and you can see in what direction things are likely to move. I may add that Ld. Normanby is greatly blamed for having expressed an opinion on the events in Paris. People say that in doing so, he exceeded the duties of his office, and Lord John has promised me that he would be very seriously cautioned not to do anything of the sort again. I have received a similar assurance from Lord Granville and from Lord Lansdowne.[1]

If the Prince will allow me to venture an opinion,

[1] Normanby was in fact recalled in February, 1852, being succeeded by Lord Cowley.

THE SECRET OF THE COUP D'ÉTAT

I would recommend him to rest content with things as they are, and much as he may regret Palmerston's dismissal, not to let it appear that he attaches too great an importance to the change, but to show confidence in the good will which is expressed here towards him. Lastly, please ask him to make no move for the purpose of securing Normanby's recall, for this would have small chances of success and would be likely to result in strained relations, which would impair the good feeling now existing between the two governments.

A great deal of all that has happened would have been avoided if those responsible for the conduct of affairs had had more experience—you see good intentions are not enough, they must be translated into practice.

I must revert again to what I wrote to you yesterday: I am certain that the Prince's object in employing special missions to announce his ten years' Presidency, is to give prominence to his huge majority. Now, not only would the influence of Court etiquette prevent this object being attained, but it might actually tend to belittle the announcement. It would be wise to avoid the disappointment to which this might give rise.

I enclose an article, more or less official, which

has been published in the *Globe*, in contradiction
of all that has appeared in the other newspapers.

Palmerston to Lansdowne [1]

CARLTON GARDENS, 29 *Decr.* 1851.

My dear Lansdowne,

I have cordially to thank you for your kind
and friendly letter. There is no one whose judgment I esteem higher than I do yours, and there
is no one therefore whose approval of the course
which I have pursued in the conduct of our foreign
relations can be more valuable and gratifying to
me.

Your friendship I trust I never shall lose, and
no political separation will I hope ever in the
slightest degree affect our private relations with
each other.—Yours very sincerely,

PALMERSTON.

Granville to Flahault

The following note, as may be seen by Russell's
letter of Dec. 31 to Granville (Fitzmaurice's *Life
of Granville*, i. p. 64) was sent at the Prime Minister's personal instigation. It was a curious state
of affairs. Flahault had just arrived in London
after actively participating in the *coup d'état*.

[1] In reply to Lansdowne's letter of December 24 (*supra*).

Russell had just dismissed Palmerston because he had approved it, and had appointed in his place Granville, who might be presumed to have regarded the *coup* with disfavour. Under such circumstances we should expect to find Flahault somewhat coldly received in Governmental circles; but, on the contrary, he became at once (to the exclusion, as it would appear, of the official British representative, Normanby) engaged in a series of highly confidential negotiations, both with the new Foreign Secretary and with the head of the Government!

For an account of the conversation which ensued with Granville, see Fitzmaurice's *Life*, i. p. 66.

LONDON, *Dec.* 31/51.

My dear Monsieur de Flahault,

I have such complete confidence in your frankness and in your wish and *power* to maintain the good understanding between France and this country, that I am very anxious to have a little conversation with you, on matters which I should not like to broach to those who, like Walewski or Normanby, hold official situations.

Pray let me know as soon as you come to town, when I will immediately go to your house. —Yours very truly, GRANVILLE.

III
AFTER THE COUP D'ÉTAT
(1852)

III

OUR correspondence for the year 1852 deals with the aftermath of the *coup d'état*, more particularly as it affected the positions of Flahault and of Morny. We left the former as the guest of Lord Lansdowne at Bowood, and the latter as Minister of the Interior in Paris, where since December 2 he had controlled almost unchecked the internal administration of the country.

Morny's letters to Flahault during this interesting period have almost all been preserved, and they are supplemented by two documents which, though without signature or date, can be readily identified as from the pen of his friend the Comtesse le Hon. His *dictature éclairée* was not everywhere viewed with the same enthusiasm which it provoked amongst the Comte de Laubespin and his friends. He had jealous rivals who were determined to oust him if they could—notably Persigny, who, though instrumental in the *coup d'état*, had for some reason been left out of the new Government, and Maupas, whose ambitions pointed to something greater than the prefecture of police.

It was not till later that Morny adopted as a tribute to his mother the "Hortensia" for his crest, but contemporary writers inform us that he was even now inclined—from his half-brother's point of view—to presume too much on their relationship. Moreover, some newspaper articles had appeared in England on this subject, and the President viewed with apprehension anything which tended to undermine a position at the moment none too secure.

Morny had his own grievances against the President. The wholesale decrees of banishment affected many of his personal friends, and Louis Napoleon showed no inclination to listen to his pleas on their behalf. There was also the decree by which it was proposed to sequester to the State all the property which the Orléans family still held in France, and this too was persisted in by the President in spite of Morny's opposition.

Madame le Hon's somewhat diffuse letter of January 14 shows, perhaps better than anything which has yet been published, how these various factors contributed to the final rupture between Morny and the Prince. It is interesting to compare and to note the differences between her account and that given by Maupas of the same events in his *Mémoires*, pp. 560–68.

Morny resigned on January 21. The letters which follow show that Maupas was in error in stating (*Mémoires*, p. 563) that he did so on the 14th, though it is no doubt true that he had had at least one stormy interview with the President before he took the final step. Fould, Rouher and Magne left the Government at the same time, and two days later they were replaced by Persigny, Abbatucci and Bineau.

Meanwhile Flahault had been working quietly but persistently in England on behalf of Louis Napoleon. For many years past he had been intimate with the British Prime Minister, Lord John Russell. He was on terms of friendship with the ex-Foreign Secretary Lord Palmerston, as well as with his successor Lord Granville. His daughter, as we have seen, was married to the eldest son of the President of the Council, Lord Lansdowne, whose opinion then, as always, counted for much among his fellow Whigs. No one could have been in a better position than Flahault to smooth the path for Louis Napoleon, and it must have been largely due to him that the *coup d'état* and its consequences were, after some show of hostility at the outset, received with comparative equanimity on this side of the Channel.

But Flahault's position was not without its difficulties. He had, as we have seen, been unwilling to take part in any Government under the name of a Republic; he was nevertheless ready to accept a seat on the Senate which had just been instituted. The situation, however, from his point of view was soon to undergo a change. He had long since perceived that any chances which the Orléans family might have of returning to France were remote; he was nevertheless still bound to them by ties of sentiment if not of affection. He had foreseen the danger of an attempt to confiscate their property, and had endeavoured to guard against it by his counsels. The passing of the confiscation decree of Jan. 22 therefore went far to alienate his sympathies from the President, and the ousting of Morny decided him for the time being to take no part in the affairs of his country.

A comparison of dates shows that the letter which follows was written immediately after Flahault's conversation with Granville already referred to (*supra*, p. 232), and that it reflects, no doubt for the benefit of the President, the views which Granville had expressed.

AFTER THE COUP D'ÉTAT

Flahault to Morny

LONDON, *Saturday evening*
[*Jan. 3, 1852*].

My dear Auguste,

We got back from Bowood to-day and I found your letter, which I was very glad to receive. I am delighted to hear that the ceremony [1] took place, because it gives a religious sanction to the will of the people, and since you were responsible for it, I am particularly glad that it went off so well. But what delights me most of all, is that the Prince got back to the Élysée without misadventure.

I shall make use of the report [2] which you have sent me; I have already had it sent through M. de Saux to the *Morning Post*, and through one of my friends to the Prince.[3] I have not given up hopes of softening the latter's opposition, but it is a harder task than I had anticipated. I fancy that he is influenced from some French source, and I should not be astonished to find that Léon

[1] The *Te Deum* at Nôtre Dame, where, on January 2, the President returned thanks publicly for his re-election.

[2] On the casualties of the *coup d'état* (*supra*, December 25, 1851). It would seem that it was M. de Saux who, under the guise of "Our Paris Correspondent," was made to father the *Morning Post* version of this report.

[3] Evidently the Prince Consort, who displayed throughout these proceedings a marked hostility to Louis Napoleon.

Faucher and his friends were in some way responsible. All the same the feeling here is changing, particularly as regards the events of the beginning of December; people begin to realise that the only way of bringing things to a successful conclusion was by taking strong measures such as those we were forced to employ.

I hope that great moderation of language will be enjoined on our Foreign Office, for nothing can be worse than to threaten violent action which it is not intended to put into effect. I fancied from my conversations with several of the ministers, that anxiety was shown lest we might intervene in too strong and decided a manner as regards the border states, such as Switzerland and Piedmont. I think I was able to reassure them, but I did not hesitate to say that it seemed to me that we were bound to insist on the removal to a safe distance from our frontier of the revolutionary centres which shelter political refugees of all nationalities. But while I did my best to reassure them, I made a point of standing up for what I hold to be our rights in these matters.

Good-bye, my dear friend, let me hear from you as often as you can. If, as you say, you miss me, I miss you just as much; but in Paris it is just as bad, for there I am cut off from my belongings.

Well, we must try and arrange all this. When you have an opportunity, give my respectful duty to the Prince, and, my dear friend, do not forget the affection which I shall always bear towards you.   F.

Lord Grey came to Bowood, and was there during the last three days of our visit. He is very much afraid that we shall not restore to our country all her liberties. I told him that he could rest assured that if there was one man in France who was ready to give her back those liberties, that man was the President, but that if he were to do so, he would run the risk of losing all his popularity.

Good-bye again.

Lady Palmerston to Madame de Flahault

Madame de Flahault and Lady Palmerston had been for many years on terms of the closest friendship.

Some of the newspapers had attributed Palmerston's fall to certain communications which, it was alleged, Flahault had made from Paris to a British Cabinet Minister. Madame de Flahault had evidently written to Lady Palmerston to explain that this report was devoid of foundation, and had sent her a copy of Flahault's letter to the *Times*, printed below.

BROADLANDS, *Janry. 3/52.*

My dear Cts. Flahault,

I am very much obliged to you for your kind letter, and to M. de Flahault for his explanation, which it was very amiable of him to wish to make; but we never attach any importance to newspaper reports, and always suppose them to be fabrications, if we know no other reason for believing them to be true.

I have been very much vexed at this extraordinary business, and more I can assure you on public grounds than private ones, because I feel that this sort of *esclandre* about nothing, is very hurtful to Lord John and to the Whig party. I *know* that Palmerston is quite free from blame of any sort; and that therefore whenever the Parliament meets, he will prove himself to be perfectly free from the slightest imputation, as he did on the Greek question; but then the triumph which one feels at defending oneself from enemies becomes a source of pain when one has to prove such an old friend as Ld. John to be entirely in the wrong. I must say that I never was more pained at any thing than at his conduct and look

242

upon it as one of the most rash and indiscreet acts I have ever known him to commit. However this may be a Wife's opinion, and therefore I don't expect you to trust to my words now, but the meeting of Parliament will I suppose explain all things.

I am sure dear Ld. Lansdowne will have been very much vexed at these circumstances, in whatever quarter he may think the blame lies, and I am very sorry that he should have any worry of any sort.

Believe me, dear Mde. de Flahault, yrs. very sincerely,   E. PALMERSTON.

What a triumph the President has got! The Valeskys look in great spirits at this result and the fine scene at Nôtre Dame.

Flahault to the "Times"

January 5, 1852.

To the Editor of the *Times.*

Sir,

I find on my return to town that the statement published in the *Times*, of a private correspondence having taken place between a Cabinet Minister and a person of influence in Paris, has obtained considerable credit, and is supposed to allude to me; and a morning paper having even mentioned my name I think it due to others, as well as to myself, to declare that the report is totally unfounded.

When I was in Paris (which I left on the 25th of December) I had no correspondence or communication, direct or indirect, with any person in office here.

May I beg the favour of you to insert this letter in the *Times?*

I have the honour to remain, Sir, your obedient humble servant,

COMTE DE FLAHAULT.

* Flahault to Morny

[LONDON, 7 *January* 1852.]

My dear friend,

Since the English newspapers have attributed to me some share in the information which led to Palmerston's dismissal, I thought it well to send a formal contradiction of this rumour to the *Times*. You know how little we anticipated this event and the surprise which it was to us; it was brought about solely by the imprudent divulgence to Normanby on the part of Turgot of the information which he had received from Walewski.

Since I have heard nothing more of the project

244

for an extraordinary mission in the matter of the Election,[1] I suppose that it has been dropped, and I am glad. Although (as I have already told you) I am convinced that the relations between the two Governments and between the two nations will not be impaired by the events of December 2nd, it is no use pretending that these events have not produced a bad effect at Windsor; or that the Queen, who from her Coburg connection has warm sympathies with the inhabitants of Claremont, is not at the moment very ill disposed towards the Prince. She is a constitutional sovereign in every sense, and so far as politics are involved she will act according to the advice of her ministers; but in the matter of her personal relations, you may be sure that she will not fail to show ill humour, or at the least her lack of sympathy. If I happened to be the person entrusted with this mission, there would be the further incentive of showing her disapproval of the course which I have taken. If I alone had been concerned, I should not have much minded, for I am always ready to bear the consequences of my own actions; but while I should no doubt have come in for my full share of the displeasure which would be occasioned, the chance would

[1] Cf. Morny's letter of December 26 (*supra.*)

not be missed of attacking the President and the great achievement by which he has saved France.

If Walewski reports, as I feel sure he will do, the manner of his reception at Windsor the other day, he will confirm all that I have now told you. I suppose that the Constitution will appear in a few days,[1] and if my name is included among the Senators I shall go and take my place.

The report which you sent me[2] has been published in the *Morning Post* and in the *Herald;* the *Times* finds some difficulty in making up its mind to publish it—a circumstance which is not hard to understand, since it gives the lie to all the exaggerated accounts which have appeared in this newspaper. M. de Saux, who sent it to the *Morning Post*, seems to have made a mistake in the figures, for he gave the number as 315 instead of 215. Why does this report not appear in the French newspapers?

I think you will see a change in the tone of the *Times;* I don't say that it is going to become friendly, but it will perhaps become less slanderous and less hostile than it has been. Ellice denies most emphatically that he has influenced its policy in any way. He told me that he had

[1] The new form of Constitution was published on January 14.
[2] On the casualties of the *Coup d'état* (*supra*).

written to Thiers to urge him not to come to England—though at the same time he offered hospitality should his advice not be followed—but he made him appreciate how much the condition of affairs was altered by the seven and a half million votes, and how much the size of the vote would weigh in the opinion of this country. I still believe that Thiers is better in the *Place St. Georges* than in banishment; the idea of banishment is distasteful, and in this country they can only recognise two alternatives—in their view a man must either be free or under sentence.

Good-bye, dear friend, I embrace you with all my heart.

I know from a sure source that the Queen has sent Van de Weyer to Brussels, in order that he should consult King Leopold as to the line which should be taken as regards France. This Van de Weyer is a curious little fellow; though seemingly ingenuous, he is cunning and treacherous. It is strange that he once provided a passport for Louis Napoleon, and that he has now just given one to the Prince de Joinville for his recent escapade! Unless I am much mistaken King Leopold's advice will be in favour of the maintenance of amicable relations with the President.

THE SECRET OF THE COUP D'ÉTAT

*Flahault to Queen Marie Amélie

The Flahaults, as we have seen, had been in the past in close relations with the French Royal family, and Madame de Flahault as well as her eldest daughter, Lady Shelburne, continued on friendly terms with the ex-Queen of the French up to the time of her death. The copy from which the following letter is printed is that which Lady Shelburne mentions (*infra*, Jan. 14) as having been sent her by Flahault, and it is probable that his letter was written at his daughter's instigation.

Our archives do not contain a reply, so we are left free to guess whether the communication remained unanswered, or whether the reply was of such a nature that its preservation was not deemed desirable.

LONDON, 11 *January* 1852.

Madam,

Your Majesty has often allowed me to approach you directly, and I venture to hope that you will not think it presumptuous if I once more take that liberty, although I write on matters which are purely personal to myself. I may perhaps remind you, in support of my plea, of the twenty years during which I was in the happy position of

being able to give to you proofs of my duty and
devotion.

Since I returned to this country, on the 25th
of last month, I have been hesitating whether I
should take this step, not because my heart did
not prompt me thereto, but because from what I
heard of the impression made on Your Majesty
by the occurrences in Paris I feared that I might
be considered tactless and that you would be dis-
inclined to listen to what I have to say. Nevertheless after giving the matter my best consideration, I have come to the conclusion that a man
inspired by honesty of purpose, who can look back
without shame on the line which he has taken in
all the troublous times through which we have
passed, has a right to be favourably heard.

I will say at once, Madam, that when I went
over to Paris at the commencement of November,
I foresaw that a crisis was coming. I hoped that
it might be possible to avoid such a violent and
dangerous upheaval as that which has since taken
place, by re-establishing between the President
and the leaders of the majority in the Assembly
the good will which certain very regrettable mistakes had impaired. Unfortunately fresh and
even more regrettable mistakes nullified my efforts
and brought in their train the necessity of the

measures which were taken on the 2nd of December. Your Majesty will permit me to add that it was against anarchy and against the authors and abettors of the Revolution of 1848 that these measures were mainly directed.

But your Majesty's view of the conduct of those who took part in these events will naturally depend on a due appreciation of the circumstances and the necessity of such measures, and I am quite aware that it will not be identical with mine. Nevertheless I can say with a perfectly clear conscience that, just as in 1830, my course of action was determined by the love of my country and the wish to save it from the great perils which threatened, and that no feeling of ambition or of personal interest influenced my conduct.

I do not expect you, Madam, to listen to me with indulgence, but nevertheless I feel that I must assure you that if, by once more taking part in the affairs of my country, I have contracted new obligations, I do not feel that I have been in any way false to the allegiance I bear to your Majesty, which nothing will ever destroy.—I am, with the most deep respect, Madam, your Majesty's very humble and very obedient servant,

COMTE DE FLAHAULT.

AFTER THE COUP D'ÉTAT

*Morny to Flahault

OFFICE OF THE MINISTER OF THE INTERIOR,
14 *January* 1852.

I wish you were here with me. I have been much worried by serious matters about which I have not dared to write—they may entail very grave consequences for the country. I shall do my duty to the end, but so long only as I can do so with honour.

It is in circumstances like these that one feels the need of a trusted friend like you.

I have unfortunately no time to write to you fully at this moment. I am just off to the Council and I am overwhelmed with business.

I embrace you all. AUGUSTE.

*Comtesse le Hon to Flahault

[PARIS] *Wednesday* [*Jan.* 14, 1852].

Dear Monsieur de Flahault,

My daughter has been trying to give herself airs; she has sent off her letter without letting me know, or I would have added a few words to tell you how grateful I am for your kindness to her. She will wear out her bag by continually opening it and fingering all the pretty things which it contains.

251

THE SECRET OF THE COUP D'ÉTAT

I am addressing this letter to Mr. Small, in order that I may speak freely to you. It would be as well if you were to let me have some address which would not attract attention, and which I could use when necessary.

Since your departure, you will have seen by the newspapers that your friend has continued to manage everything in his department with the greatest success. His firmness, his cleverness, and his true understanding of the country's needs have won general approval.

Some little time ago M. de Maupas gave the President a list of *exilés* in which were included a number of perfectly inoffensive people (all Orléanists) whom you know well. There was Piscatory, who left Paris directly he had been released from prison, announcing that he was going home to "plant his cabbages," as he realised that he must keep quiet; Daru (Paul), who is sometimes more and sometimes less reasonable, but who on the whole has done nothing very bad; Saligny, who as far back as the 3rd or 4th of December went to the Government and said he would make no move, and kept his promise; Vitet, who took the same line of action—and many other perfectly inoffensive people. M. de Morny objected strongly to these men being banished, and their names

252

were struck off the list. He attempted also to get Rémusat's and Lasteyrie's names struck out, but Mme. Rémusat's violence made this impossible, and her husband's name was therefore retained on the list—which was finally left as you saw it.

For a time the Ministers thought that the President would forget about these people, but when the deportation decrees were being signed, the list of *exilés* once more made its appearance and the President, before the decrees had been countersigned, told the Ministers that he wished them to sign at the same time a decree for the confiscation of the Orléans property. I need hardly tell you that the principal Ministers strongly objected and tried to show the President that he had no right to do anything so unjust. For their part, they said, they would never sign; indeed they threatened to resign at once and to refuse even to sign the banishment decree. After a few minutes the President consented at their suggestion to refer the matter to Messrs. Troplong, Menars [*sic*], and a third jurisconsult,[1] and to abide by their decision. The Ministers, being convinced that these three lawyers would settle

[1] Troplong, Meynard and Rouher were the three jurisconsults of the new régime.

253

the question in the sense they desired, determined to sign the banishment decree—believing that they would very soon be able to sign another decree permitting their return.

It was on Friday last[1] that this took place. The next day Fould went to see the President on the business of his department, when, just as he was leaving, the latter said to him, "I have thought it over, and I shall not consult those three gentlemen. They might possibly not take my view of the matter, and I have made up my mind to confiscate the Orléans property." Upon this Fould reminded him of his promise, on the strength of which the Ministers had signed an act which they cordially disliked—for *exilés* never forget those who officially countenanced their banishment. He pointed out that the President was breaking his word, that he himself as well as M. de Morny and his colleagues would refuse to make themselves parties to the transaction, and that their portfolios would be immediately handed in. Fould then came to my house, as did also the others (Magne and Company), who all approved of his action.[2] M. de Morny called on the President,

---

[1] *I.e.* on January 9.
[2] According to de Maupas (*Mémoires sur le Second Empire*, p. 560). Fould was all this time secretly working against Morny.

in order to show him that it was a question which concerned himself much more than the Orléans family; that it would ruin him; and that the country would strongly condemn such a step for which no justification could be shown. He besought him not to be persuaded into a course of action which would appear to be prompted by a spirit of unnecessary vengeance, and reminded him of the whole-hearted devotion and affection which he himself had shown towards him. It would, he said, cause him distress to be obliged to send in his resignation, but he neither could nor would sign an act of this nature. The President retorted that this was childish nonsense, that after a few days nobody would pay any attention to the matter, that although he would be distressed to part from him politically, he was determined on this measure; he would, however, think it over once more. This was on Sunday.[1] The four Ministers,[2] after much discussion, which would be too lengthy to repeat, ended by agreeing that it was best to accept the lesser of two evils, and that it would be necessary to invite Persigny and de Maupas to join the council, on the condition that they would oppose the confiscation proposal.

[1] January 11.   [2] *I.e.* Morny, Rouher, Fould and Magne.

In order to arrange matters as quickly as possible, this suggestion was made and accepted, and although these two schemers said that they regarded the matter in a different light to the Ministers, they undertook to withhold their support.

The President then agreed that he would consult a lawyer (probably one of his friends), and M. de Morny persuaded him to add that the discussion should take place in the presence of the Four, with Persigny and Maupas also present. This briefly is the story.

The President is determined to have a Ministry of Police as well as a Secretary of State: I wonder what he will do with Turgot and how it will all be settled. Our friends will have nothing to do with it. To understand the position of affairs you must know that Persigny and Maupas are trying to undermine the authority of our friend in all kinds of ways, in the estimation of the President as well as in that of the public. They are not only determined to come into the Government themselves, but they wish to get rid of M. de Morny, to which the President would not be averse. He must be his own master, and will brook no opposition. M. de Morny's popularity, the directness and absence of flattery which characterise him, do not suit the President. It is just as I said—having made his *coup*, he intends to be supreme. I cannot tell you all the little things which would prove to you that such is the case. If M. de Morny were to remain with the two schemers, it would merely delay his resignation, and he would have to go a little later on, while the public would think that he had been obliged to do so by the influence and the intrigues of these two men. Should a man who has rendered such splendid services as he has done to his country, who has behaved so nobly, leave the Government in such a manner? In my opinion—No. He would be lowering his position, and indeed it is already lowered from the fact of his having identified himself with those two people.

In his place, I would leave when the change of Ministry takes place. But I believe that it will be an evil day when he goes; people will lose confidence, credence will be given to all the foolish schemes attributed to Persigny and the President, and though I don't wish to put too high a value on our friend, I believe the President will be dealing a blow to his own power and to its duration. This is my opinion. The Ministers say that they will go with M. de Morny; but I expect if the confiscation question does not arise again they will remain—with the two newcomers. It would be well if we could make them pledge themselves against it—they do not, of course, feel the matter as deeply as does the Minister of the Interior. Persigny wants the Interior and advises M. de Morny to take Foreign Affairs—but this he has refused to do.

I need not tell you that the President has not once thanked our friend for all he has done. He pays not the slightest regard to him.

He wants me to write and ask you for your advice. Should he stay on with these two men, on the understanding, of course, that the confiscation proposal is dropped? They would be so pleased to have got into power, that they might not work so much against him. My own view is that he is no longer wanted, and that since Persigny desires the Interior he will sooner or later be forced to go; while, by putting up with these two men (whose action will have compelled his resignation), he will seem to have been merely clinging to office. M. de Morny wants to know if he ought, in the interests of the country and of the President, to endure this state of things as long as he can. Please answer all this.

Everything which has happened in the last fortnight was foreshadowed in a long conversation which I had with Persigny and from which I drew my own conclusions, though M. de Morny refused to accept them. On that occasion he went so far as to say that the Rhenish provinces should be annexed in order that the powers might see that they had a master before whom they must quail; that we must have done with all these royal families and all the old parties; that the President was the man to carry out the regeneration of society; and the Tuileries was the place from which the world must be made to tremble, etc. etc. It was the language which an escaped lunatic from Charenton might have used. He added that none of the present Ministers understood the position, although M. de Morny did so better than the rest; that his own mission was merely beginning; that all he prophesied had come true, and that he would, in collaboration with the President, carry out the policy which he had originated, etc. etc.

To-day I had a long talk with Bacchiocci. He is a good fellow, without jealousies; he does not boast, is not ambitious, and is a good judge of men. It would take too long to report the whole of our conversation, but he said to me, "Let them include Persigny; he will do less harm inside the Government than outside. He exercises great influence over the President, since they hold the same political views. We shall soon have some surprises. I am of a philosophical disposition and ready to take things as they come, but the poor President will not rest content with his splendid position, he will spoil it. It is an infamous action to try and confiscate the Orléans property and it will not be popular; I am well aware that the intention is denied at the moment, but he has curious notions. Morny must be patient, and must rise superior to his troubles. The President does not realise that he is indispensable, because he does not think any one could be so: looking at the matter from a detached point of view, I say that the President will not govern wisely, and Persigny is a bad counsellor—and a dangerous one, from the fact that he is at one with him in all his schemes. But anyhow it would be best that they should let him join the Government."

I have told you very briefly everything which might help you to appreciate the situation. What would you do in our friend's position? Would you go when the two others come in, or would you wait? Have you read what he said at the Hôtel de Ville banquet?[1] It seemed to me to be quite

[1] The reference would seem to be a speech made by Morny at a banquet given by the Préfet de la Seine on January 4.

friendly to the President, but Persigny has told him that the President did not like it, because his words seemed to mean "He is my brother, I know him and protect him." The excitement and anxiety which M. de Morny's resignation will be sure to cause would not be so great from the fact of his having remained on with these two men, and they are not thought much of, I can tell you. Since, therefore, it seems to be certain that he will eventually be compelled to go, should he not have some regard for his own interests and take the dignified exit which now offers? It will be a case simply of returning to private life on the plea of his health. I can assure you that he is much changed, one cannot stand indefinitely so much business combined with worry. He will become a well-paid senator[1] and will live in peace.

The President, who had agreed that Thiers should remain in Brussels, has, without telling M. de Morny, caused an official request to be made to the Belgian Government that he should be sent away; which has, of course, been done. I believe he is in London, but this fact will not be of much use to the Royal family, who since the second of December have determined to hold no

[1] A salary of 30,000 francs attached to the office of senator under the new constitution.

further communication with France. The Queen and Mme. la Duchesse d'Orléans have sent me, through the King of the Belgians, the most tender, friendly and grateful messages possible, thanking me from the bottom of their hearts for my letters, etc. Changarnier has refused to go to England, for he wishes to avoid becoming the lion of the hour in London. He has asked permission to come to Belgium, and has given an assurance that he would take no sort or kind of part in what is going on. General Le Flo has used the most vulgar abuse about the Government, Bedeau much the same. Madame de Rémusat has shown such violence that most people have thought it right that her nephew should be sent away.

M. d'Haussonville was at Brussels, where, in conjunction with M. Thomas, he produced a report of a most hostile nature against the President. The King of the Belgians asked them to leave Belgium, and they are now in Holland. D'Haussonville was so violent that his own family hoped that he would go abroad. These outbursts are peculiar to him and I cannot believe that they have been inspired by the Prince.

I have written at length, but I had to tell you everything in order that you could form a judgement on the question which my neighbour has put to you. I have expressed it all very badly, but you know how time presses, and if I have not written legibly, this must be my excuse!

Please reply under cover to the address of Mme. d'Herenemont, Rue de la Pepinière, at the corner of the Rue de Courcelles, No. 120.

I press your hand, dear M. de Flahault, in all affection. My neighbour asks to be excused for writing to you by the hand of his friend, and begs your forgiveness.[1]

Lady Shelburne to Madame de Flahault

BOWOOD, *Wednesday* [*Jan.* 14, 1852].

I hope you don't approve of all these French *exilés*. It seems to me such mistaken policy and so at variance even with the President's own promises, which limited the exercise of his arbitrary authority to the interval between the *coup d'état* and his re-election. Surely, with such a majority, he could bear the presence of such men as M. de Rémusat at Paris—what a bore they will be here too!

Good-bye, dear Mamma—I must be off to snapdragon, an attempt at jollification for Clan's[2] birthday.

---

[1] This letter is without signature.
[2] Lord Clanmaurice, the present Marquis of Lansdowne, who was 7 years old that day; b. 1845.

THE SECRET OF THE COUP D'ÉTAT

I wrote to Papa in such a hurry last night that I forgot to thank him for having sent me his letter to the Q[ueen] of the F[rench].[1] Will you do so for me?

Russell to Flahault

CHESHAM PLACE, *Jan.* 16, 52.

My dear Flahault,

If you have no engagement perhaps you would call here at ten o'clock this evening.

If that does not suit you, pray come here before 11 to-morrow morning.—Yours truly,

J. RUSSELL.

The "Times," January 16, 1852

The following extract from the *Times* will serve to indicate its views (referred to *infra*) with regard to current events in France at this time.

THE FRENCH MINISTER OF THE INTERIOR

A pupil of the school of the État major, he obtained a sous-lieutenant's commission in 1832, and proceeded to Africa, where he made the campaign of Mascara and of Constantine. Of the bravery, coolness and energy of M. de Morny

[1] Of January 11 (*supra*).

there can be no doubt whatever. He was wounded under the walls of Constantine and was honourably mentioned in affairs, for which he received the reward dearest to a French soldier's heart— the *croix d'honneur.* In the military service M. de Morny remained till 1838, when he left it to engage in a commercial speculation—the manufacture of beetroot sugar, which he had commenced on a large scale in Auvergne. The delegates of the sugar interest soon appointed him their Secretary, with a view to defend the interests of the trade. The superior manner in which he explained and enforced their views in a clever pamphlet caused him to be ultimately elected president of the Society. In 1842 he first became a member of the Chamber, and frequently spoke in a manner to excite attention, from his coolness and aplomb. But although a certain ability and energy cannot be denied to M. de Morny, no one supposed him to be specially cut out for a parliamentary life, or for a great minister of State. To every man acquainted with Parisian society in the five years from 1843 to 1848, it was well known that M. de Morny was more deeply engaged on the turf, at the Jockey Club and the gambling table, and in the foyer of the Opera, than in Parliamentary business. His coolness, courage and quick faculties no one doubted. He was an excellent judge of horse flesh, understood écarté well, and could criticize an opera or a ballet with accurate science—but no one believed him to know anything about, or to care anything for, Parliamentary government.

Lady Shelburne to Madame de Flahault

BOWOOD, *Jan.* 18*th* [1852].

Lord L. goes to town for good on the 26th, and, as Shelburne talks of going even sooner, I should not like to be left alone. Moreover, I have always that dreadful feeling that Papa will be going back to Paris and that the sooner I go to town the more chance I have of seeing him. I cannot help hoping, however, that he will not belong to that Senate of whose doings, good or bad, we shall never have any account.

I wish some of you would tell me why M. de Rémusat is exiled. Is he merely obnoxious, or has he been conspiring since the *coup d'état?* for he was not among the first arrested, at least I think not.

Ld. L. goes to town for another Cabinet to-morrow. Poor man—he has a sad life of it just now! I wish he too was well out of the mess.

AFTER THE COUP D'ÉTAT

What line does Lord Beauvale take in the Palmerston business? I am glad you went to Brocket, for it must have pleased him.

Telegram

Comte de Flahault from Auguste de Morny.

Dear friend,

Put off your departure for some days and do not leave before you hear from me. I will write you to-morrow.

* Flahault to Morny

The Orléans family still owned large estates, of a value of some 300 millions of francs, in France. By a twofold "decree," promulgated three days after Flahault's letter was written, they were (1) compelled to sell the whole within the space of twelve months, and (2) ordered to forfeit to the State the endowment which had been made in Louis Philippe's favour on his accession to the throne in 1830. This enactment—popularly described at the time as "le premier vol de l'aigle"— was the cause, or, as some said, the pretext, of Morny's resignation a few days later. Rouher, Fould and Magne left the Government at the same time, while Montalembert—one of the most reputable amongst the President's early adherents —ostentatiously retired from the *commission consultative* to which he had just been appointed.

This letter is taken from a copy kept by Flahault, and there can be no doubt that it was intended rather for the eyes of Louis Napoleon than for those of Morny. It will have been noticed that Flahault had already been privately apprised (by Madame le Hon) of the President's determination. He was therefore well aware that he was dealing with no mere "club rumour." His reasoned arguments against the proposal would, moreover, have been wasted on Morny, who disapproved of the measure almost as much as he did himself.

LONDON, *January* 19, 1852.

My dear friend,

Your *message* reached me yesterday, Sunday, and I have put off my departure, which was to have taken place this morning. I am sorry for it, since it is important that I should get back to Paris before the opening of the English Parliament, for I have some rather important matters to discuss with the Prince—anyhow, I shall wait two or three days for the letter you are to write me.

Yesterday at White's they were saying that

EMILY, COUNTESS OF SHELBURNE

AFTERWARDS MARCHIONESS OF LANSDOWNE

(From a miniature by Thorburn)

the President was planning the confiscation of the property of the Orléans family, and I need not tell you the kind of comments to which this gave rise. I hope that it is a false report—one of the wicked libels of which the English papers are full. I cannot believe that a Prince so just and so strong, a man of so noble and generous a nature, could ever countenance the idea of such an act of spoliation, which would disgust all honest men. I can remember the effect which was produced by a similar step taken in 1814 by King Louis XVIII. against the Emperor's family; it disgusted me then, and I cannot believe that the Prince would run the risk of creating such a deplorable impression.

The principle of confiscation was recognised up to the end of the Empire as part of the penal code of France. The framer of the present law[1] had himself suffered under its hardship. Since confiscation usually followed the death penalty, it hit the innocent successors rather than the guilty party. Provision was therefore made that the head of the State might temper the hardship, by disposing of the property confiscated in favour

---

[1] *I.e.* the law of March 2, 1832 (Art. 22), which enabled the King to retain possession of property which had belonged to him before accession to the throne.

of the father, mother, widow, children or other relatives, by blood or adoption, of the person so condemned.

Besides this, confiscation could only take place when expressly authorised by law, and the law only gives that authorisation in the case of a Frenchman who has borne arms against France. Book III. of the Penal Code cites every instance in which this penalty may be inflicted; it could certainly not apply to any of King Louis Philippe's sons, who since the February Revolution have offered no resistance to the steps taken against them. Besides this, confiscation has been formally and for all time abolished by Article 66 of the *Charte Constitutionelle*, and this abolition has been so generally accepted, that a measure such as this must be considered as a formidable attack on the rights of property.

You may be quite sure that if the Prince were to decide on a step of this kind he would alienate public opinion both in France and in all Europe —and, in point of fact, if one comes down to a matter of sordid calculation, the property in question is not worth the trouble which would be involved.

Since the 10th of December, 1848, Prince Louis Napoleon has won, by the strength, honesty and elevation of his conduct, the good opinion of all honest men, and it would be very sad to see all this lost through what would appear to most people a deed of petty and shameful vengeance. But, as I have already said, I am loth to believe that there can be the smallest foundation for these rumours.

Russell to Flahault

This letter, read in conjunction with Lord John Russell's note of January 16, indicates that Flahault was being at this time closely consulted by the Prime Minister as to the attitude adopted by the British Government towards the French President.

The conversation here referred to must have been that which took place between Queen Victoria and the French Ambassador on the occasion of the latter's visit to Windsor (see Flahault to Morny, January 27). It would appear that Her Majesty was unable to conceal her distaste of the President and his works, but that the Prime Minister (at Flahault's instigation) had done his best to pour oil on the troubled waters.

[LONDON] *Jan. 20, 52.*

My dear Flahault,

I find all this bother, of which you spoke to me, is owing to the Queen's having forgotten to use the words which she intended.

273

THE SECRET OF THE COUP D'ÉTAT

She has written down for me this morning the words she intended to have used, and Granville can communicate them to Walewski,—omitting this little fact of the Queen's having omitted, from nervousness, some of them.—Yours truly,

J. RUSSELL.

Morny to Flahault

[PARIS] 20 *January* 1852.

My dear friend,

I asked you not to come, because it will be better that you should not be mixed up with, nor credited with any share in, the things which are going to happen. I have quite made up my mind not to remain in the Government. I have a thousand good reasons for this course, which I cannot specify to you, because I have not the time, and besides I do not like to trust them to the post; but you may be sure that I have not come to this conclusion without a strong sense of its necessity. Your arrival here before a crisis in which I shall be the person principally concerned could only have bad consequences.

You are aware of all that has happened in regard to the matter with which your letter just received deals. The idea has not been given up —the storm will burst one of these days and will have awful consequences. I bitterly regret this on account of the Prince and of the country. I have done everything in the world, and gone so far as to risk the loss of his confidence, in order to prevent it: it is because I find that loyalty and devotion, when accompanied by candour, are not always appreciated that I do not wish to remain longer. Heaven save you, with your fine character, from the fate of being a man without power in the Government. This will become a Government of nonentities, there will never be room in it for a man of character and independence.

I will write fully in a few days. You will perhaps come to Paris, but, believe me, your presence here will do no good, it will merely give rise to a thousand rumours.

I embrace you with affection.   A.

Comtesse le Hon to Flahault

[PARIS] *Wednesday* [*January 21, 1852*]

Dear Monsieur de Flahault,

I have only a few minutes before the post goes in which to tell you of my neighbour's[1] regret that he cannot write to you, but he is very much occupied. He will probably leave the Govern-

[1] Morny.

275

ment to-morrow. His resignation has been accepted. I can assure you with the utmost confidence that this was the object aimed at. For some time past he has been blamed for working against the Confiscation project; he was told that every one knew about it, that he would not be able to achieve his object, and that he would be sorry for his action. He was shown also some articles in the *Times* dealing with the question of his and the President's parentage[1]—this very much disturbed the President. No attempt was made to keep him and I repeat it was intended to get rid of him. You know, for I have often told you, how much jealousy there has been and how loth was a certain person to accept his decisions or act on his advice. His help was wanted to carry out the *coup d'état*, but there it ended: and I may tell you that you also are wanted no longer. These are the real feelings of this man, who has none of the finer qualities and who, you may take it from me, is little worthy of your esteem. His sincerity and apparent courtesy serve to conceal all sorts of evil propensities. The reason my neighbour urged you not to come

[1] I have been unable to find any such article in the columns of the *Times*. Madame le Hon probably had in mind the paragraph printed on p. 264, which, as will have been seen, is far from complimentary to her friend.

was that you should not be mixed up with all the intrigues that are going on, they would be unworthy of you and would disgust you. Come when you wish, but allow me to urge you to think well before you do so. You are able to keep clear of everything which is going on—you should take advantage of this circumstance and wait.

Drouyn de Lhuys is going to have Foreign Affairs, Persigny the Interior, Maupas will be Minister of Police and Casabianca Secretary of State. Then Arnaud, Fould and some others stay on.[1] This is the position at the moment. To-morrow either I or my neighbour will write. I have only five minutes to spare just now. Will you be able to read my writing? A thousand pardons and a thousand kind messages.

Lady Palmerston to Madame de Flahault

BROADLANDS, *Jan.* 21 [1852].

Dear Cts. Flahault,

I was delighted to hear your account of Thiers' *imprudent* declarations—If he would only go on with *this assertion*, it would do so much good, that the harm of all his other chatter would be neutralised. I am only so afraid that Ellice,

[1] Turgot remained Minister of Foreign Affairs in the new administration, and Fould did not stay on, though he subsequently became Minister of State.

Chas. Greville, or some others, should try to close his mouth and tell him that the acknowledgment of his intended *coup d'état* is the best service he can do the President. I have no doubt of the fact—but in general people do not, or say they do not, believe it. When Mr. de Flahault goes to Paris, it would be a great object to get some proofs of this conspiracy published.

People in England are really so foolish and absurd in their abuse of the President that one feels quite ashamed of their want of sense and of their letting themselves be so led by the *Times*. Besides, whatever people may think here, the French are certainly the best judges of their own affairs, and if 8 millions have approved his *coup d'état* and have thought it necessary, I don't see what right we can have to make such a clatter. One of the foreigners who was at Claremont at the time of the *coup d'état*, told me the Prs. de Joinville said, in her despair and lamentations at the loss of her hopes, "Et moi qui croyais être à Paris le 20"—but pray don't quote me for anything.

I am very sorry not to see you and M. de Flahault, but I can understand that you have both much to do.—Believe me, Yrs. very sincly.,

E. PALMERSTON.

The Cravens went to town to-day.

AFTER THE COUP D'ÉTAT

* Morny to Flahault

[PARIS] 23 *January* 1852.

My dear friend,

You will read in the *Moniteur* of the change in the Ministry[1] and of the very serious occurrence which has brought it about. I can only hope with all my heart that it will not have such bad results as I had feared. I cannot tell you how much all this distresses me. Everything looked so promising. Success seemed assured. It is the English newspapers and their insinuations[2] which are responsible for the trouble.

You will understand why it was that I besought you to remain in London. You could not have prevented anything which has occurred, and your presence here must have encouraged every sort of rumour, which would have distressed us both.

As far as I am concerned, I quit with the good opinion of the outside world, and with sorrow that the approval which has been accorded to my actions should now be turned into disapproval of the poor P[rince]. But still I am on quite good terms with him, and I shall certainly afford him no cause for complaint, either in my conduct or in

---

[1] The names of the new Ministry were published in the *Moniteur* of January 22.

[2] *I.e.* on Morny's relationship to Louis Napoleon.

my words. We have travelled far since the 2nd of December!

Good-bye, my dear friend. I embrace you with affection. Be careful how you write to me —one must be very much on one's guard with a man like M. de Maupas at the head of the Police.

And now, my dear friend, you must make up your own mind whether or not it would be wise for you to come here. You know how happy I should be to see you at any time. You may rest assured that when I saved you from the command of the Garde Nationale[1] (without sacrificing thereby your generous and splendid devotion) I was thinking of nothing but your own interest and your own good name, which I value above all else.

AUG.

* Morny to Flahault

[PARIS] 26 *January* [1852].

My dear friend,

You seem to have misinterpreted my recent appeal that you should not come to Paris. Believe me, it was only from affection and devotion to you that I made it. You know that I

---

[1] It would seem that this must have been offered to Flahault immediately after the *coup d'état.*

have occasionally in the past spoken to you very frankly on the subject of the P[rince]. Since the 2nd of December I have come to understand his character better still. In the first place, he has no real friendship for any one; less perhaps for me than for others—and then my peculiar position is an annoyance to him, and yours makes the matter still worse.[1] I have kept a good many things from you. At the time when you were thinking of joining the Government, you were animated solely by the desire to help the Prince, and to strengthen his power, and you no doubt thought that your suggestion would be agreeable to him. But there was nothing he would have disliked more, and he would never have consented to it. He put up with my presence very unwillingly, and my very services were irksome to him. He has never been more unfriendly towards me than he was at that time. He is mistrustful and ungrateful, and only likes those who obey him slavishly and flatter him.

When he wanted your help in England, he asked for it, and he has never forgiven your refusal.[2] He could not find any one else for the

[1] Morny is of course here alluding to the curious ties of relationship which united the three persons in question.

[2] *I.e.* of the ambassadorship in London (*supra*, p. 127).

2nd of December, so he made use of me. I risked
my life; I accomplished my task, but what
matter; I am in the way; I am neither a slave
nor a sycophant, so I am cast off as useless!

And what could you have done if you had
come to Paris and taken part in the events which
were impending? Any word you might have
uttered would have been exploited, repeated and
distorted. They would have said either that
you had inspired the decrees, or that you were
strongly against them; that you had come either
to stop me from leaving the Government, or to
induce me to leave it.—People are so stupid!
Anyhow, you would not have been able to change
the course of events, of that you may be sure.
Therefore, under the circumstances, what was the
good of coming over and being mixed up in this
business? It was in the hope that none of these
things might touch you that I kept you away,
and I felt sure you would approve of my conduct.
It was for your sake and not for mine, for you
know well that both your companionship and
your advice are very precious to me. Now that
all is over, come if you think it advisable to do so.
The Senate is about to be installed; you and I
are invited to join. Shall you accept? If you
refuse, I shall do the same. I have a good

mind to refuse in any case—I have had enough of political life, especially with a man like the Pr[ince]. I should very much like to know what you are going to do. On the whole I do not feel that you could honourably accept; and to myself the idea is intensely distasteful.

Good-bye again, dear friend. I feel very sad and deeply wounded. It seems a far cry from the triumph of two months ago to my disappointment of to-day! But for all this I embrace you as affectionately as ever.   AUG.

* Flahault to Morny

LONDON, 27 *January* 1852.

My dear friend,

I did not, as you imagine, misinterpret your appeal that I should not come to Paris; but I was anxious to know the reasons which prompted it, and from what you now write I think them mistaken. I do not mean to assert that I could have prevented these occurrences, but no one can say that I might not conceivably have done so. In any case, you could have been certain that I would have done nothing which would have had the effect of damaging my good name, nor should I ever have given you any advice which could have hurt your own.

283

THE SECRET OF THE COUP D'ÉTAT

You say that you have kept many things from me. But why? It seems to me that in our relations nothing should be kept back —especially where matters of such importance are involved. I am convinced that the request that I should not come did not originate with you, and, my dear friend, I have some fear that you are even now acting under influences which are hostile to, or at any rate unfriendly towards, the person in question.[1]

Pray be on your guard against this, and do not, just because certain things have upset you, take such a gloomy view of everything. That some people should like flatterers, should look askance at those who show independence of spirit and resist their wishes, that they should find such men inconvenient, good God, surely this is the case with all men in authority and with many who are not! Believe me, it will be best to show friendly feelings towards the President and to make him *forgive* you for the services you have rendered; they have indeed been great enough to weigh heavily upon him! You did well to leave the Government, but you must not flatter yourself that they will be grateful to you for doing so at Claremont. They dislike us both,

[1] This seems to be a veiled allusion to Madame le Hon.

284

even more than they dislike M. de Persigny. You must bear in mind that your attachment to the President and love of your country are the only excuses for what you did on the 2nd of December. Let these motives always remain your inspiration.

You must accept the office of Senator, for this will afford you the opportunity of still being useful. As for me, I am differently situated. My career is over. If I could wipe out the 2nd of December, I would willingly do so. After all, I had but little part in it, and if it had not been for you I should not have been there at all. Recent events have dispelled the illusion that we inaugurated a happier future for our country on that day. But you did not then hold the views which you now express, and it was largely your views which determined my opinion and my line of conduct.

I am sending you, open, a letter for the President [1]—it is for your eyes only, and remember, dear friend, that the secret contained in this letter is not your own and that you must on no account divulge it to any one. When I remember the way in which affairs of State were treated by some of your friends and all the gossip there has been about things and about persons, I cannot conceal

[1] The letter was not sent; *vide infra.*

from you my apprehension that confidential matters may have been repeated, and that these indiscretions may have been the cause of irritation and have produced some evil effects. In a position of such trust and importance as that in which you found yourself it was essential to preserve the utmost secrecy.

Now that it is all over, I do beseech you not to allow those who are near you to make themselves a centre of opposition and to work against the man for whom you have shown so great a devotion. Rest assured that, however excellent your intentions, you were badly advised when you wrote to me not to come over. My affection for you was such that I was bound to act as you wished, but I did so very regretfully.

I embrace you with all my heart.   F.

P.S.—There is a story going about here, as to which I should like to know the truth, so that I may, if possible, contradict it. It is said that you arranged that Lord Normanby's box at the *Français* should be taken from him, in order that you as Minister of the Interior might have the use of it. I immediately asserted that I did not think such a thing possible, that it would have been most unlike you, with your character and your good manners. Can it be that your subordinates took so improper a step without your knowledge? Talking of Lord Normanby, I think it is unlikely that he will return to Paris.

You are no doubt aware that the English papers tell a story about your dealings with Mme. d'Osmond;[1] I give no more credit to this one than to the first, and I class it with another in which I am supposed to have visited M. Molé, and to have been summarily shown the door!

Good-bye once more. Send your letters for me to Dumarest and Ducoing.

P.P.S.—The newspaper brings us the list of Senators. I therefore keep my letter,[2] which is

---

[1] This story had been published by the *Times* on January 26 under the heading, *Gossip of the Paris Salons*. Madame d'Osmond had a salon where opinions adverse to the new régime had been very openly expressed. Having been warned by the Minister of the Interior that this must not continue, she ceased to invite her male guests. The ladies, however, continued to be no less explicit in their comments, and it was alleged that their hostess had received a polite intimation from Morny to select whichever of her country residences she might most prefer, since the President would no longer tolerate her presence in the capital.

In the same paragraph it was said that Flahault, when calling on Molé, had observed that two ladies who were in the room had immediately left it when he entered, while their host remained seated. Upon his asking Molé why they had done so, the ex-Minister replied that they had left the house for the same reason that he would have left it had he not been unable to move owing to the gout!

[2] *I.e.* his letter to the President mentioned above, in which he had apparently asked that he should not be nominated to the Senate.

no longer required, and am very glad that it is so. Perhaps, as you say, the Prince preferred that I should not be nominated, but at any rate he must have been quite certain that I could not accept. As far as you are concerned, I cannot see that there was anything against it, and I am very much afraid that some of your neighbours [1] must have shown imprudence in their talk; it is quite clear to me that they wished to put you on bad terms with the President. Do try, I beseech you, to imbue them with calmness and moderation, for nothing could do you more harm than if either you or I were to show a spirit of opposition or to speak of the President in a hostile or ill-natured manner.

Give your mind to your business concerns. You have played a leading part in saving France from a great peril; your name is associated with all the important measures which have restored order, and perhaps it was in reality most fortunate that you were forced to bring to an end the work which you had only undertaken out of loyalty; if you take my advice, you will not utter a single word which would justify people in suggesting that you had a grievance.

[1] *I.e.* Madame le Hon.

AFTER THE COUP D'ÉTAT

Morny to Flahault

[PARIS] 28 *January* [1852].

My dear friend,

I cannot go into all the details, but the Prince has displayed towards me such heartlessness, and so little nobility of character, that I have become disgusted and have refused to be a member of the Senate. I took upon myself to declare that you also would not accept nomination. I think I have done what you wish. I would prefer to have nothing more to do with this Government. I feel affection for the man himself, but contempt for his Government and for the people he has round him. The best of princes are thus made; they prefer toadies to honest men.

Tell me if you are coming over, or if I am no longer to expect you. I should much like to come and see you, but with these suspicious people it would be thought that I had come in order to see the Orléans princes, to whom, as you know, I have scarcely given a thought. Ah well! But after all I am very glad to have a quiet time.

I embrace you with affection. AUGUSTE.

I keep my mouth shut. I show no sign of opposition, but I am sad and grieved to see so brilliant a prospect destroyed.

THE SECRET OF THE COUP D'ÉTAT

Flahault to Madame de Flahault

Wednesday [? *28th January* 1852, LONDON].

My letter would be useless, as I am happy to find by the lists of Senators just published [1] that the President had well judged of my intentions. From Auguste's not being named, I suppose that he also would not have accepted, or that his language or that of his *entourage* or *voisinage* may have been imprudent or violent. I mean to go on as I have done, that is, to be impartial to the P[resident], rather favourable than otherwise, where it is not impossible to be so. In what I did I had no selfish views. I thought it right to help to extricate my country from great difficulties and dangers, and only hope that the P. will pursue his task with success. . . . We dine at Lord Lansdowne's and go after to the John Russells'.

* Flahault to Louis Napoleon

LONDON, *January* 30, 1852.

Monseigneur,

At the time I was thinking of returning to Paris, Lord John Russell begged me to give you

---

[1] On Monday, January 26, therefore this letter, dated Wednesday, must have been written on the 28th.

an account of one or two conversations which I had had with him. These related to the Parliamentary debate which is about to take place in regard to Palmerston's dismissal. Since this was due to matters which concerned France, Lord John was specially anxious to give you an assurance that, whatever might be said, you could be sure that there would be no change in the friendly relations between the two Governments, and the two countries. If you will permit me to give my own opinion, I think you can rely on this promise.

Perhaps, Monseigneur, you will also allow me to take this opportunity of saying something about myself.

I beg you to believe that on the 2nd of December last, I placed myself once again under the Standard, to which my early years had been devoted, with a very real sense of pleasure; and, when I had the honour of taking my leave, the kind words by which you were good enough to show your approval of my efforts were quite a sufficient reward for the poor services which I had been so happy to render. If since that time I have found myself in disagreement with certain measures which you have thought fit to adopt, and have made up my mind to return to a position of obscurity and inactivity, I feel that I must

give you the assurance that I have only done
what I consider right in the circumstances, and
that my gratitude towards you is such that
nothing would have been more repugnant to my
ideas or to my feelings than to have shown any
active opposition or, still more, any marked dis-
play of disapproval.

My conduct during the *coup d'état* has given
grave displeasure to the former Royal Family,
and has earned me the marked enmity of all the
Orleanist party. Pray, Monseigneur, do not think
that I flattered myself with the hope that I
might lessen these feelings in the slightest degree
by the course which I have pursued. I know the
world too well to cherish such an illusion; but
for this reason I am all the more anxious to
make it impossible for any one to accuse me
of ingratitude.

Rest assured, Monseigneur, that I shall go on
with the task which I came here to fulfil, that
I most earnestly wish for your success, and that
from the bottom of my heart I regret that I
cannot have the honour of contributing towards
it by my services. Rest assured also that I shall
always be ready, as I was on the 2nd of December,
to afford you proof of my devotion, should it be
in my power to help you.

COMTE DE FLAHAULT

Aet. 60

Pray, Monseigneur, be good enough to accept the assurance of my deepest respect.

FLAHAULT.

* *Louis Napoleon to Flahault*

ÉLYSÉE NATIONALE,
11 *February* 1852.

My dear General,

I was very glad to hear from you, for I cannot forget the proofs which you have given me of your loyalty, and it has been to me a source of deep regret that anything should have interrupted the good and sympathetic relations which have existed between us.

It was no less a source of regret to me that a step which I considered indispensable should have forced Morny to resign, for I have the greatest affection for him.

I hope, my dear General, that you will allow me, as soon as circumstances may permit, to add your name to the list of the Senate, for no one has a better right than you have to such a position, and no one would be able to bring to its counsels a more enlightened judgement, more authority or more patriotism.

I am content with the ministerial pronouncements in Parliament, but nevertheless I cannot help realising that the rumours of war, ridiculous as they may be, have actually been put about and encouraged by the English Government.

I am most anxious to see you and to repeat to you the assurances of my deep attachment and friendship.

LOUIS NAPOLÉON.

* Memorandum by Flahault of a Conversation with Palmerston

Flahault's account (*infra*, p. 308) of his proceedings at this time show that this conversation took place immediately before his return to Paris in February, 1852, and that his memorandum was set down, in order that he might be prepared for his subsequent interview with the President. The sequel shows that Flahault's arguments, backed though they were by Palmerston's powerful support, were not sufficient to shake the President in his decision.

The question of the validity of the gift or endowment, which had been made to Louis Philippe in 1830, came before the Seine tribunal, and when this court showed an inclination to pronounce upon it in a sense favourable to the Orléans family, the President at once referred the matter to the *conseil d'état*. The *commissaire* and the *rap-*

porteur were both against the Government, but the much-discussed decree was in the end passed, though only by a bare majority of that body.

February 1852.

I called on Palmerston and told him that I was proposing to spend a few days in Paris, and, knowing the feelings which the Prince held towards him, I felt sure that the latter would wish to hear his views as to what is going on in France, and what people in England are thinking about us. "There is one measure," I added, "as to the effect of which I have unfortunately nothing to learn, for it can be perceived only too easily. What distresses me most is that there is nothing to be done, for I cannot see any possibility of annulling the decree by which the Orléans property has been confiscated. My views are perhaps influenced by the attachment which I feel towards this family; but I should much like to know what you think of this measure, for you, at all events, are not suspected of any sentiments of this nature."

[Lord Palmerston.] An Englishman cannot be a good judge of this matter in its legal bearing. Nevertheless, I have read the arguments on both sides, and I was much struck with that advanced by Berryer: namely, that the accepted rule (by which the personal property of a Prince who succeeds to the throne has to pass to the State) applies only to one who succeeds to the crown by right of inheritance, and not to one who ascends the throne as a result of a revolution —for the obligations of such a one towards the State can only commence after he has accepted his new position. But however this may be, it is unfortunate that the Prince President should have taken this step whilst he was enjoying absolute powers which are by their nature of a temporary character. These powers have been conferred on him for the purpose of providing for the needs of the country, pending the establishment of the constitution, which it was his duty to provide, and the urgency of the matter was not so great as to prevent its being deferred for submission and adoption by the properly constituted authorities. In my view, this measure has had a deplorable effect, and one which will prove lasting in its nature. It will never be forgotten, and will always remain a reproach which can legitimately be brought against him. It is considered wrong, even by people who are not at all friendly to the Orléans family; and since it is not justified by any action on the part of those against whom it is directed, nor by any judicial decision, it is held to be an act of personal vengeance. But I am not at all of your opinion that the mischief is irrevocable, and should the Prince appoint a commission of the most eminent legal authorities with a view to their making a report as to the legality of the step, and should their report declare it to be *ultra vires*, I consider that he would by revoking the act earn the highest commendation.

[M. de Flahault.] Allow me, my dear Palmerston, to differ from you on this point. I need not tell you my opinion of the measure in question, since it was one which compelled me most regretfully to part from the Prince and to give up working for his cause. Nevertheless, I could not advise him to follow the course which you now suggest, for this would seem to show weakness; the unpopularity of the measure would still cling to the Prince, while all the credit for its abrogation would fall to the Commission.

[Lord Palmerston.] Excuse me. In the first place, I do not consider it a sign of weakness for a Government to abandon a course on which it has embarked in the conviction that this course was unjust or illegal. Nevertheless, I am not insensible to the last argument which you adduce; but, granting this, what is to prevent the Prince from obtaining the information and advice of the most eminent men privately, and why should he not then on his own initiative repeal or amend his decree, just as he made it? We have in one of Sheridan's comedies (*The Rivals*) a phrase which perfectly expresses the position: "*An affront handsomely acknowledged becomes an obligation.*" [1] At any rate, if I might give advice to the Prince, I should not hesitate to say to him: "You have done a thing which has pained your best friends; it has alienated from you men who wished you well, and whose services it was your interest to retain; it has roused against you public opinion all over Europe, and from the manner in which it was carried through it threatens to cause anxiety as to your attitude towards the rights of property"; and I should add, "*The best thing that you can do is to back out of it.*" I am ready to admit that this plan may have some slight drawbacks, but they will be transient, whereas perseverance with the measure would entail lasting anxiety and blame. It would become, though in a less acute form, what the execution of the Duc d'Enghien was to the Emperor.

---

[1] This passage, as well as those printed in italics (*infra*), is quoted textually in the original document.

AFTER THE COUP D'ÉTAT

[M. de Flahault.] I have been told that the Prince was induced to act as he did for two reasons. First, the belief that the Orléans princes were using their money for the purpose of corrupting the English press; and, secondly, that the hostile spirit shown against him since the 2nd of December by the Queen and Prince Albert was attributable to their influence. Although this rumour does not rest on good authority, I think it is probably true.

[Lord Palmerston.] I only know of one case of corruption actually practised on the *Times*, and this was merely to obtain its silence, and £10,000 had to be paid.[1] I doubt whether there is any foundation for this accusation against the Orléans princes. Why should they have wanted to pay the *Times?* It was always ready enough with its violent and angry attacks, indeed its pages were full of them.

As to the Queen's attitude, her friendship for King Louis Philippe dates from her earliest years. He had, as you are aware, with all his cunning, a great affectation of good nature, and he treated the young Princess with what seemed almost fatherly affection, an affection to which the

[1] It would be interesting to know to what incident Palmerston was here referring.

Queen fully responded. Their friendship was
impaired for a time by the Spanish marriages,
but was revived by the misfortunes which followed
the February Revolution, while the ties of relationship which resulted from the Coburg marriages
gave it still greater force.

Moreover, she conceived a warm affection for
the children, and this wretched decree which
takes everything from them must have been felt
deeply by her, since it hits those who are nearly
related to her husband. You may be sure that
this decree (which has the appearance of a piece
of gratuitous persecution directed against the
Orléans family) has done more harm to Prince
Louis Napoleon and has been a greater injury
to his cause than the Orléans family itself could
have been, even if it had employed the whole of
the fortune of which it is now deprived to work
against his interests. *I repeat it is much better
that he should back out of it than persevere in it.
A Government always gains credit by repairing an
injustice.*

We then went on to talk of the Constitution
and of the liberties which it would, when established, confer on the country. "It seems to me
impossible," said Lord Palmerston, "that the

system at present in force can long continue, without the most deplorable results for the Prince. A country may submit to the deprivation of all its liberties while it believes itself to be threatened with a danger so great that it can only be saved by a strong hand, but it must not be imagined that it will be ready to make a similar sacrifice when it no longer has this fear. The man whom it had hailed as its guardian will then be considered its oppressor; and the worst of it will be that the Prince himself will have no means of feeling the change in public opinion, since all those organs which were against him have been suppressed. If he has been moulding his action on the policy followed in the time of the Emperor, I think that he has scarcely realised the difference between those days and the present. At the time when the Emperor became head of the State, a liberal system in the true sense of the word had never been experienced in France. The people had only seen, on the one hand, absolutism tempered by the traditions of the old Monarchy, and, on the other, the wild and bloody licence of the various governments which had succeeded the Revolution. They were only too glad to feel themselves under the protection of a hand which, while it brought them glory, was both strong and just. But what has happened since then? For 33 years France has enjoyed, under parliamentary institutions, all the liberties, both material and moral, which a people could desire. She has been kept fully informed of events and has thus become accustomed to participate in the conduct of her own affairs. Do you imagine that the country will long be satisfied with an Assembly whose speeches are not reported, or with a press which is dumb, or very nearly so? I cannot believe it."

[M. de Flahault.] In my view, what France needed above all else after the 2nd of December was the re-establishment of authority. She was like a horse which has become wicked and vicious; she needed a powerful and strong bit, but at the same time a hand clever and light enough to guide her without making her restive.

[Palmerston.] *Depend upon it, he must relax or it will not do.*

I asked him next if he thought that the absurd rumours of war and of projected invasions were put about by the Government. He replied that he did not think so, but that he had no doubt the Government would take advantage of them, in order to get Parliament to pass certain measures of defence which he had himself urged for some time past. He pointed out that all the great European Powers had increased their military establishments; that since 1815 England alone had progressively reduced hers, in accordance with the spirit of her institutions, and also as a measure of economy; he knew, however, that the increase in the regular forces would be limited to three or four thousand men; the House of Commons would be asked to vote the necessary funds for the mobilisation of the Militia for a fortnight or three weeks, but this force could not be used abroad and was intended solely for home defence. In 1815 it amounted to about 40,000 men for Great Britain and 20,000 for Ireland, while to-day (by reason of the growth of population) it might be estimated at 100,000 men. But on the whole he thought that these steps would tend rather to allay the apprehensions which the press is endeavouring to excite, than otherwise.

Lord John Russell and Lord Lansdowne, with whom I have also discussed this question, spoke to me in a similar strain.

Flahault to Madame de Flahault

The date of this letter is fixed by its political allusions. On February 20, 1852, Lord John

THE SECRET OF THE COUP D'ÉTAT

Russell's Government was defeated on Palmerston's amendment to the Militia Bill, and replaced by an administration under the leadership of Lord Derby. The ex-Foreign Secretary thus had his revenge on those who had turned him out only two months before. Flahault was evidently writing from Paris, where he had come in the hope of persuading the President to give up his Confiscation proposal.

[PARIS] *Sunday* [? *22 February* 1852].

I have had two long conversations, the last of an hour and a half—very friendly, but with no effect. There is a conviction that what has been done is politic, legal and just. I intend to return to you before the end of the week. . . . I am afraid there will be a good deal of difficulty to form a Tory administration. Why was Lord John opposed to make the Militia available for all general operations when its services might be necessary in the country? I cannot understand how it could have been of any use without that, and I must say that unless there are other motives unknown to me, such as a feeling in the country against it, I should have voted for Pam. . . . Pray write a line to Christie's to say that Auguste will not sell his pictures this year.

AFTER THE COUP D'ÉTAT

** Flahault's Conversation with Louis Napoleon
on February 21, 1852* [1]

When I was in London a short time after the *coup d'état*, I received a letter from Morny in which he told me that the Emperor had allowed himself to be persuaded by some of his intimate friends to seize the property which King Louis Philippe had appropriated when he accepted the crown at the time of the Revolution of 1830. Strictly speaking, the action of King Louis Philippe had been illegal, for the property in question was in the nature of an endowment, and the custom was that when a Prince thus endowed ascended the throne, property of this kind should merge in the State. Still, admitting that from this point of view the King's action had in 1830 been illegal, it became so no longer when he ceased to occupy the throne.

It was clear to me that those who advised the Emperor to pursue this course hoped by means of this ill-judged proposal to so disgust the Ministers then in office that they would leave the Government. Amongst those of whom I speak was Persigny, who had been by an error of judge-

---

[1] This account was dictated by Flahault to his daughter Georgine, probably about the year 1865.

ment left out of office, Abbatucci, etc. etc. Morny kept on saying how much he regretted my absence at this juncture, and I decided to go back to Paris; but before doing so I found means of seeing Palmerston, with whom I had a long conversation. He was in complete agreement with us, and did not hesitate to say that no greater mistake could have been made by the Prince President, and that he felt certain that his action would have the worst possible effect on all honourable men. I listened carefully to all he said on this matter, and when I went home I put it down on paper, in order that I might show it to him, and thus be certain I was not putting words into his mouth of which he might not approve.

The next day I left for Paris, and I was able to see the President at the Élysée on my arrival. Just before seeing him I met Persigny, who expressed to me the hope that I would join the Government. I answered him quite plainly that the contemplated measure was not one which made me anxious to do so, and then I went in to see the Prince, who received me very cordially and said he hoped that I should now consent to join the Senate. I replied that the step which I heard he was about to take would of itself be an insurmountable bar to my acceptance. Then began a conversation about this measure, which lasted for two and a half hours that day, and remained even then unfinished. The Prince said that we could take it up again the next day, and appointed a time for the purpose. It was in vain I employed every argument which I could think of myself, as well as all those which I had drawn from my conversation with Palmerston. I did not forget to mention that since I was afraid the Prince might think that my own arguments were biassed by the attachment I still felt for a Prince whom I had served for 18 years, I was determined that he should know how his action was regarded by a man who was generally supposed to have been rather hostile than otherwise towards King Louis Philippe.

I will not attempt to recapitulate all this long conversation in detail, indeed my memory would not admit of my doing so; but towards its close I besought the Prince to put the matter before a commission drawn from amongst the members of the bodies (the Senate and the Council of State) which he had just constituted. I pointed out that should this commission pronounce in favour of the measure—a point on which I felt more than doubtful—he would at all

events have acted according to law and would
no longer bear the sole responsibility for an
enactment which in my view was a deplorable
one. He answered that the arguments I had
used had produced a sensible impression on him,
and if the matter had remained secret they would
have caused him to hesitate; but the thing was
known, and if the outcome were unsatisfactory
the only effect of following this course would be
that he would incur the charge of lack of consistency. I replied that far from this being so,
I was convinced that if he appointed this commission, and announced in his own way that
the method by which King Louis Philippe had
appropriated property which should have re-
verted to the State was held to have been quite
illegal; that he was himself inclined to question
the legality of the manner in which it was proposed to reappropriate this property; that (since
it is as much the duty of all governments as it
is the desire of the governed to secure impartial
justice) he had decided to submit the question
to a commission qualified to pronounce on such
a matter—then, I added, "I am far from thinking that any one could accuse you of weakness.
I believe, on the contrary, that the column in the
Place Vendôme which was erected for your uncle's

statue would not be considered lofty enough to support your own."

It was easy to see that these words produced considerable effect upon him, but he would not give in, and there followed a silence of some duration. At length I said to him sorrowfully, "Well, Monseigneur, I regret from the bottom of my heart that you persist in this unfortunate plan. I have no hesitation in saying that you will also regret it when it is too late, and that it will be for you what the condemnation of the Duc d'Enghien was for your uncle."

"Oh," said he, "that was a very different matter."

"Yes, Monseigneur, just as murder differs from robbery."

These words must have made an impression on him, for, several years afterwards, when Lavalette returned from Constantinople,[1] he repeated to him our conversation, employing the very words which I have just set down.

In fairness I must add that he showed not the slightest sign of displeasure at the language I had used.

[1] In 1853, when M. de Lavalette gave up his ambassadorship at the Porte.

THE SECRET OF THE COUP D'ÉTAT

Anonymous to Flahault

[29 *February* 1852.][1]

You have betrayed the secrets of a family whose misfortunes you should respect.[2] Moreover, I am informed that the Duchesse d'Orléans has closed her door to you—this is the treatment which a wretch and a coward like you deserves.

You may tell L. Napoleon that he is a thief and a murderer, and that the time will come when his life and those of his accomplices will pay for those whose death he has caused.

UN ROUGE.

To Monsieur le Comte de Flahault,
    Champs Élysées,
at the corner of the rue de la Réunion.

Morny to Flahault

Morny, after his resignation of the Ministry of the Interior, was frequently spoken of in connection with the Presidency of the new *Corps Législatif*, and Maupas in his Memoirs mentions that the post had been actually promised to him by the President. This does not, however, appear to have

---

[1] Postmark.
[2] "Vous avez trahi les secrets d'une famille que vous devez respecter la douleur," etc. It would seem that this letter cannot have been written by a Frenchman.

been generally known at the time, whence we may perhaps infer that Flahault's hints on the subject of discretion (*infra*) were not altogether wasted on the ex-Minister.

It may be observed that the reasons given by the President for the withdrawal of his offer by no means tally with those given by Maupas. The prefect of police states (*Mémoires sur le Second Empire*, p. 599) quite openly that this was the result of a plot engineered amongst Morny's colleagues, in which Prince Jérôme was persuaded to join.

Morny's feelings under the circumstances may be well understood, and that Flahault shared them may be seen by his reply—the only letter in which he displays any bitterness of feeling. Both father and son were, however, soon to be completely reconciled to the Prince President.

[PARIS] *March 2* [1852].

My dear friend,

Here is the letter which I have received from the Prince. You can form your own conclusions. I will not allow myself to add to it a single word:

"My dear M.,

"I have been for some time much worried, for nothing is more painful than to be torn between one's affections on the one hand and political necessity on the other.

"Here are the facts. At the time you left the Government I wished to nominate you for the Senate, but this you did not desire. Later on, wishing to show my trust in you, I offered you the post of President in the *Corps Législatif*, and you accepted it. When I made this offer, I thought it one which was consistent with my policy, for it enabled me to show my gratitude to one who had helped me on the 2nd of December, and who by doing so had unreservedly thrown in his lot with mine. Nevertheless, the decrees of January 22nd have (though I was unaware of it at the time) altered the position of affairs. The Orleanist party, knowing that you had resigned on account of these decrees, conceived the hope that if you became President of the Chamber it would help their interests. I scarcely credited this at first, but yesterday I read an intercepted letter addressed to the Duchesse d'Orléans, written by a person of good position, in which the following passage occurs:—'Our hope lies in the nomination of M. de Morny for the Presidency of the Chamber. The President may somehow disappear from the political scene, and we may then be sure that the whole-hearted support of

M. de Morny will be given to your Royal Highness.'

"I do not attach to this information more importance than it deserves. Nevertheless, since my aim is to constitute myself, in so far as I can honestly do so, the ultimate hope of all parties, I perceive with regret that at the moment your appointment would defeat my object. It is hard for me to have to say this, and I should perhaps have scarcely had the courage to do so, if it had not been that you told me the other day that you were not very anxious for the position of President of the Chamber. For you will believe me when I say that nothing would please me better than to prove to you the sincerity of my affection. Any other appointment—an embassy at St. Petersbourg, at Vienna or at Madrid—anything which might suit you and which would not impede the course of my administration, would be entirely satisfactory to me. So think it over, and please also pity me, for nothing could be more painful to me than to be forced to separate myself to some extent from my closest friends. Nevertheless, pray believe in my friendship.

L. N."

So here is a promise definitely made, and broken on account of a letter from a person un-

named, in which it is assumed that I would have
accepted this appointment in order to help the
Orleanists. This is the reward for true devotion!
I feel very little regret for the Presidency, as
you know better than any one; but I must own
that the wrong the Prince has done me and his
lack of confidence have hurt me greatly.

Now, my dear friend, take the first opportunity
for the sale of the pictures—there is no longer
anything to prevent it, rather the reverse. You
see, my dear friend, that I had cause to regret
your departure.

I embrace you with great affection.   AUG.

* *Flahault to Morny*

LONDON, *March* 3 [1852].

My dear Auguste,

I have this moment received your letter of the
2nd, and I come back to my old opinion, that all
Princes are alike and that usurpers are the most
worthless of all.[1] You may be sure that the

---

[1] *Que tous les princes se ressemblent et que les illégitimes sont encore
ceux qui valent le moins.* The phrase, as will at once be seen, is capable
of translation in two different senses, Flahault, however, was not
amongst those who believed that Louis Napoleon was not the son of
Louis Bonaparte (cf. his letter to Morny of May 4, 1849). Moreover, for obvious reasons, he would not, even if he had believed the
President to be illegitimate, have been likely to stress this point in
writing to Morny. It seems clear, therefore, that he uses the word
"illégitime" as the antithesis to "legitimist."

COMTE DE MORNY

(From a portrait in water colour, c. 1851)

action you took on the 22nd of January will not, in the eyes of Claremont, efface the memory of the 2nd of December, while at the Élysée it will cause that day to be completely forgotten—but after all what does all this matter to you? You were inspired by a feeling of affection towards him for whom you risked your life, or at any rate your freedom, and if he shows no gratitude, so much the worse for him! Such action will not win over to him many men of honourable dispositions, nor will it earn him many acts of devotion. He may perhaps obtain the assistance of men such as those who now surround him and serve his ends, but his reputation will not be enhanced nor will he gain the country's trust.

You are aware how doubtful I felt as to whether you should accept or refuse the position of President of the *Corps Législatif;* there was much to be said on both sides of the question. But as to the appointments which the Prince now offers you abroad, I have no hesitation in saying that nothing in the world would persuade me to accept any of them. If he can bring himself to believe, on the suggestion of a third party, that you might under certain eventualities betray his cause for that of his enemies, he would be equally capable of believing that you would betray him in the

319

interests of the Court to which you might be accredited. Good God, how different he is to his uncle! and how wrong I was in my estimate of his character, even on the occasion of my last interview. My advice to you would be to remain simply and solely a member of the *Corps Législatif*, to show no spirit of opposition, to support in a straightforward manner such proposals and laws as may seem to you to be good, and to work against such as seem harmful to the country's interests; to see fewer people, to announce that you will push no person's interest, because you have no relations with any one in the Government, and to maintain the utmost reserve in your language and, when you speak of the President, to be distant though respectful.

As far as I am concerned I am confirmed by your experiences in the decision which I had already taken to keep out of everything. At Claremont they could not be less well disposed towards me than they are, but even if this feeling became less marked, I should never enter into relations with the Orléans family. Never, in spite of all the services which I rendered to them, have I enjoyed their confidence, and I cannot see that anything that I have done justifies the resentment which they have shown against me. At the same time I shall keep clear of all that goes on at Paris. It is no place for me, since they cannot trust an honourable man. It is strange to recall at a time like this that moment when you set out from the house on the morning of the 2nd of December!

If I had been in Paris I would have urged you to keep all this business as secret as possible, for it might easily do harm to the Prince, and this at all costs must be avoided. The fact that a person has wronged you must never be an excuse for your injuring him in return. Let him cherish his grievances, but let there be none on your side.

* *Flahault to Louis Napoleon*

LONDON, 29 *March* 1852.

Monseigneur,

I have not abused the permission you gave me to write to you, and I hope you will not think it amiss if I make use of it to-day in order to express to you the pleasure which some of your recent enactments have given to me. You have employed the best means to silence the hostile press, or to make it powerless for harm;[1] the good

---

[1] By a decree of February 17, reinforced by some later ordinances, the liberty of the Press in France had virtually been destroyed. As a result only a few newspapers, wholly controlled by the Government, continued to appear.

321

effects of this policy must surely be obvious. These laws have, moreover, proved a useful weapon to your friends, who wish not only for the success but for the triumph of your cause.

Please allow me, however, to take this opportunity of mentioning the bad impression caused here by the continued presence of the *exilés*. They are received everywhere, and the moderation of their language tends to make people criticise even more severely the enactment which keeps them out of their own country.

There was a rumour here that M. Thiers [1] would, if he asked permission, be allowed to return, and people are astonished that such a condition should be imposed upon a man who has neither been tried nor sentenced. Even those who do not find fault with the principle, express the view that in the case of a Government which is both strong and just, the enactment could scarcely be justified except by absolute necessity. "Moreover," they say, "there can in this case be no such necessity, since permission to return would be granted if they were merely to ask for it."

---

[1] Thiers was still in London, where, according to Henry Greville, he had taken a house for a year. He returned to Paris in the following August.

AFTER THE COUP D'ÉTAT

You have on several occasions deigned to give your kind attention to what I had to say, and I must add that I am speaking in your interest only, since for the last two years I have been on bad terms with M. Thiers; I have not set eyes on him since I have been in England, and he would be very much astonished if he knew that I was pleading on his behalf.

* Morny to Flahault

We now find Morny once more immersed in business affairs, and it can be perceived that for the time being, such questions as the Orléans confiscation and affairs of the Near East had taken a secondary place in his thoughts.

The *Vieille Montagne* was a zinc mine, near Aix-la-Chapelle, in which he had for many years been deeply interested. It would seem that there was a prospect of securing something like a monopoly for its product. History does not relate whether the particular speculation realised expectations, but from the fact that Morny's fortunes are known about this time to have improved considerably, we may perhaps assume that it did.

The guardianship of the Christian shrines or *Lieux Saints* at Jerusalem had for several centuries been a source of contention between the Greek and Latin Churches. The Marquis de Lavalette (who was later to marry Flahault's second daughter) was at this time French Ambassador at the Porte and on February 13, 1852, he had concluded an arrangement with the Turkish Government favourable to France. His "diplomatic success" in this matter was, however, short-lived. He had no sooner left Constantinople than the Turks went back on the agreement which had been made, by granting rights to the Russians incompatible with the settlement. A fresh arrangement was made on M. de Lavalette's return, but the Russians were not satisfied, and made further demands for the protection of the Greeks in Turkey. It was this which ultimately led to the Russo-Turkish War of 1854–6.

[PARIS] *Sunday 25 [April 1852].*

My dear friend,

I was overburdened with work before I started for the sitting of the *Conseil d'Administration* in Belgium at the *Vieille Montagne*. One matter in particular took up a great deal of my time, for all the meetings were held at my house; but I shall not regret it if it eventuates, as I have every reason to hope, in the combination which will suit us, and you will not be sorry for this either. It is briefly that the solder-makers wish to make use of oxide of zinc, and so to substitute the use of our product for their own; and they propose that the Government should forbid the use of solder.

You will readily see what a blow this would give to the use of solder throughout the world, and what advantages would thereby accrue to the *Vieille Montagne* and to the zinc industry. I scarcely dare as yet to cherish this hope, but all the same the affair has made considerable progress; the solder-makers are all of one mind and I have had them at my house. They are much down-hearted and alarmed by the campaign which the Government is waging against them, and they feel that their end is near—but they would rather die with compensation than without! If all this comes out well, I shall once more be established in business just as I was in former days. I shall owe no man anything, and I shall not make the same mistakes any more; I shall emerge with flying colours and shall so arrange my affairs that I shall be safe whatever may happen. I am going to repay Coutts this very day, and I shall get my pictures sent over here; I shall sell them better in Paris than in London, for when Marshal Soult's sale [1] takes place, collectors from every country will be there.

The Court of First Instance yesterday declared its competency to try the case. [2] This from the moral point of view is a big step in advance; but it has stirred up public opinion, which is most unfortunate—the best the Prince can hope for is that people should forget. What an unfortunate idea it was! and how deep the guilt of those who put it into his head. He has no idea how much it has harmed him abroad and at home, and to what an extent he has lost a position in which all were prepared to trust him with their eyes shut.

Lavalette is back in Paris, very proud of his diplomatic success. I do not know enough about the question to form an opinion, but it appears that he found the position so deeply committed that he was unable to draw back without discredit,—he would never have taken the matter up otherwise. You must take care that Walewski is not too English, and that he does not get us into trouble with the Porte, while losing us our influence in Egypt. For what have the English done for us, in any quarter of the globe?—nothing.

[1] This sale took place on May 19, 1852. Soult had died on October 26, 1851.

[2] *I.e.* the confiscation of the Orléans property, on which the Orléans family had appealed to the law.

AFTER THE COUP D'ÉTAT

So Thiers has gone.[1]   I am delighted!

I ought to have gone myself to Brussels to-day, but I have been so unwell that I have spent the whole day in bed, and I shall not leave till to-morrow. I may perhaps come and see you afterwards.

I embrace you with much affection.   A.

* Flahault to Morny

[LONDON, (?) 28 *April* 1852.]

My dear Auguste,

I congratulate you on the success which you are anticipating in your transactions with the solder-makers. Though I confess that I do not understand their claim to compensation, seeing that they are only giving up an industry which is recognised as dangerous to those who are employed in it, nor do I understand from whose pocket the compensation is to come. Still, I rely on your ability, and I shall be charmed to see the day when my shares are to put something in my own pocket.

I should be delighted at the spirit of independence which has been shown by the Court of First Instance, if I could persuade myself that

---

[1] But not to France, for he did not reappear in Paris till August.

THE SECRET OF THE COUP D'ÉTAT

this would open the Prince's eyes to the fact that
the decree of January 22 was unjust and impolitic.
I have always felt convinced that if, as soon as
he had any doubts as to its justice, he had gone
back on his original decision, he would have
greatly enhanced his reputation, and I have not
changed my mind on this point. But, since I
am convinced that the very counsellors who
initiated or encouraged this disastrous course of
action will move heaven and earth to make him
persevere in it, I am far from deluding myself
that we have much to hope. Their object is by
such methods to force him apart from honest
people, and so to keep him entirely in their own
power—and in point of fact they have been completely successful. I am sorry, therefore, that
the decision of the court has revived this subject,
for this will unfortunately have the inevitable
result of bringing about some forcible action on
the part of the executive against the judiciary
power.[1] This will do still more harm to the
Prince in the country, for, as M. de Talleyrand
was fond of saying, France, in spite of its revolutions, is a country which supports the law.

[1] Flahault was perfectly right. The President eventually got his
way, but in order to do so he had to relieve both the *maître des re-
quêtes* and the *rapporteur* of the offices which they held.

328

AFTER THE COUP D'ÉTAT

I make my compliments to Felix [1] on the renown which he has earned by his success. With a little more success of this kind, our Foreign Affairs should be in good case. If you still do not understand the question of the "Holy Places," I will not give myself the trouble, nor you the boredom, of explaining it all again, for I think I have already done so in some detail, both in conversation and in writing.

As regards Walewski I do not for a moment believe that he is inclined to be too English; on the contrary, he seems to me to be very much on his guard against the influence which the British Government are seeking to exert in their own interest and against ours. In my opinion he carries this view rather further than is reasonable, but he has a good political brain; he understands the meaning of high diplomacy. He thoroughly realises that the Porte needs our support, but that it cannot be a useful ally for us and that it is only by agreement between all the Great Powers that the life of this moribund state can be preserved. We cannot by supporting in 1840 the interests of the Pacha of Egypt against the Sultan,[2] and in 1852 those of the Sultan against

[1] Marquis de Lavalette.
[2] Abdul Medjid had been Sultan since 1839.

the Pacha, assist in maintaining the integrity of the Ottoman Empire!

But after all, my dear friend, the thing which seems to me important for our diplomacy is that we should preserve friendly relations between the Prince and the Great Powers. It is surely inevitable that he will be impelled to make himself Emperor, and the way in which this change will be received will depend on the state of his foreign relations. You may be sure that before the question of the Holy Places had arisen, the feeling for us in St. Petersburg was very different from what it has been since. This I consider to be a point of the first importance, and you must surely agree with me. If in order to re-establish our exclusive protection of the Christians in the East, to which all the Christian powers now agree, we quarrel with the Emperor of Russia by trying to deprive the schismatical Greeks of their part in the Holy Sepulchre, and if at the same time we put ourselves wrong with England by inciting the Sultan to attack the Pacha's authority, we shall find that we have—out of lightness of heart and for no useful purpose—impaired our relations with two of the Great Powers with whom it is important that we should be on good terms.

Further I hope that the Prince will assert

himself in the direction of his affairs. I believe him to be animated by very sound ideas, and I confess that I am inspired with no confidence in any one but him.

You know that Philip never sent the cases for your pictures and that he says he knows nothing about them. If therefore you really intend to sell them in the near future you must make the necessary arrangements for their removal in good time. If you had any thought of keeping them, we should prefer that they were not sent for until after the Season, for our drawing-room will have to be repainted after they have been taken down, and this would be more conveniently done during the dead season; but you will understand that this consideration must not count if it is a question of choosing a favourable moment for the sale.

Good-bye. I embrace you.

I should like you to read the political part of this letter to the Prince.

Flahault to Madame de Flahault

The work of the *coup d'état* was now about to be completed and Flahault had come over to Paris to

see his friends and to vote for the Second Empire.
The assumption of the Imperial title by Louis
Napoleon was announced on December 2, the
anniversary of the *coup d'état*. There had been
some eight million votes for and only a quarter of
a million against the proposed change.

Flahault was still unwilling to take an active
part in the affairs of his country, and shortly after
his return to England he sold his house in the Rue
d'Angoulême.

[PARIS] *Saturday* [*Nov.* 1852].

I have found your letter on my arrival and
regret to find that you were surprised and hurt at
finding me gone. I thought I had indicated it
to you. . . . I have as yet seen nobody except
Auguste and the neighbour, with whom I dined.
Their description of the state of society is terrific.
Going into a drawing-room is alarming, for one
runs the risk of driving a number of people out of
it. I shall console myself if it drives away people
I dislike, and yet it is disagreeable to go and pay
visits under these circumstances. However, I
hope not to be long exposed to those *ennuis*.

Aug[uste] has written to the P[resident], who is
still in the country, that I am arrived and I shall
see him, I suppose, in a few days.

AFTER THE COUP D'ÉTAT

[Paris] *Monday* [*November 22, 1852*].

I received yesterday an invitation to a ball at St. Cloud, where I was very graciously received by the President. Everybody asks me if I am not come to stay, and I say that I am come to vote and only to stay a few days. I hope to be with you in the beginning of next month.

I have fought several battles for W. against those who blame him for having attended the funeral.[1] In answer to the statement that he had been authorised, it is said that he ought to have had a cold. I defend him gallantly.

I should be glad to get £1000 for the blue service.

Poor Emily's attachment for the D[uchesse] of O[rléans] blinds her. I am already considered too much as no more a Frenchman.

My neck makes me leave off and I am going to vote. . . .

[Paris] *Friday* [*November 26, 1852*].

I am just returned from St. Cloud, where I have been perfectly satisfied with a very long conversation I have had with the Prince. It is

---

[1] The Duke of Wellington had been buried on November 18. It was supposed that the President had insisted on Walewski, the French ambassador, attending the funeral, but this does not seem to be borne out by Flahault's comments.

too long to repeat in writing, but both on publick and private grounds it gave me pleasure.

[Paris] *November 28* [1852].

I don't think that the old French Parliamentary history offers a scene of more intrigue and dirty proceedings [*sic*] than what has taken place in the House of Commons.[1] It is as unlike the old English character as possible. The fact is that the moment the two great parties were broken up, trickery was necessarily the order of the day, and I should not be astonished if, to bring it to perfection, ballot in elections and the secret vote in the House should become the law.

Everybody torments me by pressing me to take part in what is going on here—legitimists, foreigners, in short, all shades. My answer is that I cannot abandon my sick daughter, but I am not approved. I hope to be with you in the first days of next month. I am never away from home without wishing to return there.

Tell our neighbour[2] that I believe he has

---

[1] There had been a great debate in the House of Commons on a motion in favour of Free Trade brought forward by Mr. Charles Villiers. From this Lord Derby's Government, which leant towards Protection, succeeded in escaping by carrying an amendment which in fact begged the question. They were, however, defeated on their budget soon afterwards when Lord Aberdeen's Government came in.

[2] (?) Walewski.

enemies at the Foreign Affairs, but that the P. is satisfied with him and knows the perfection of his wife. . . .

The following letter from Flahault to Madame de Flahault is of uncertain date. Its contents seem to justify its inclusion at this point, though it is possible that it relates to a conversation between the Emperor and Flahault to which a reference is made by Henry Greville two months later.

The "neighbour" must be Walewski, the French Ambassador in England, with whom the Flahaults were on very close terms. He appears to have had enemies in Paris, who thought him too prone to view matters from a British standpoint.

"My great friend" is clearly the Emperor. It would seem that Flahault is here recounting a part of the conversation mentioned in his letter of November 26, and that it had reference to the fear of a French invasion which prevailed in England at the time.

Cowley was now Ambassador in France, and Clarendon was for a short time Foreign Secretary-designate in Lord Aberdeen's new ministry, though the post was actually given in the end to Lord John Russell. He vacated it, however, in 1853 in Clarendon's favour.

THE SECRET OF THE COUP D'ÉTAT

[PARIS] *Sunday* [? *November-December* 1852].

Pray tell your neighbour that I have had a very long talk with my great friend, and that he is as reasonable as possible. Your neighbour would injure himself here if he was not extremely moderate in his language and conduct. [There is] great indignation against the infamous wretches who threaten all countries with revolution and all thrones with assassination, but at the same time great confidence in the disposition of the English Government to do all it can to thwart their bloody designs, and great respect and admiration for the laws and feelings which have made England an asylum for all great political misfortunes [*sic*].

Allow me at the same time to reject as very illogical all your comparisons. It would have been very unjust to have expelled one who lived quietly in England and never abused its hospitality, even if power had existed to do so; and I don't see how the boy Jones' attempt [1] could have been reproached to or attributed to his residence in any of the continental powers. I hope that none of these arguments will be made use of.

While I was expressing my view of the case

[1] The "boy Jones" was a half-witted youth who had broken into the Queen's apartment at Windsor Castle in 1840.

COMTESSE DE FLAHAULT
(BARONESS KEITH & NAIRNE)
c. 1860

to my great friend, I was startled at seeing him smile. However, I went on, and when I had finished he said, "You saw me smile! It was because what you said was exactly what I had said myself. It is very fortunate that it is so for the other Powers are ready for a crusade against England and say that what N[apoleon] I. did so much to bring about, might any day be done by his nephew."

You may say all this to Clarendon, though Lord Cowley knows it and I daresay has written it to him—say it all to your neighbour in confidence, as far as I am concerned. . . . You may say to anybody you please that my great friend is very reasonable and pacifick and friendly to England. It is of great importance to cultivate this good disposition.

Morny to Madame de Flahault

[PARIS] 17 *December* [1852].

My dear Madame de Flahault,

I am sorry that you feel distressed at the sale of the house. To tell the truth, I feel rather sad about it myself, but for reasons rather sentimental than practical. Since you are not going to come to Paris any more, was it not absurd to keep so much capital thus locked up? You would have had to spend a lot of money if you were going to inhabit the house, and unless he were actually to throw in his lot with the present Government—which M. de Flahault will not consent to do—it would really be folly to keep it, merely for the purpose of spending a few days there every now and then. On the other hand, you can now without risk employ the capital, which is once more at your disposal, for the purpose of increasing your children's fortunes.

You know my feelings as to the Emperor, and that (in my view) there are numerous reasons why M. de Flahault could honourably accept an official position. Nevertheless I do not conceal from myself that such a course might possibly not meet with approval in England; that he would be criticised for taking it by members of his own family; while he would find himself here in the midst of a new set of people who are scarcely on terms with all his former friends. The soil is new—you would yourself find difficulty in accepting all its products. The position must be a false one for some time—I find it so myself, and you would feel it more keenly still. His action during the last two years, and especially since the 2nd of December, is the real criterion and this has won universal approval. The only criticism I have to make is that there are certain people who, while admitting the immense service which Prince Louis Napoleon has rendered to his country, keep aloof from him for personal reasons. But we must let time do its work.

AUG.

Laissons faire le temps—Morny's words were to come true sooner than he can have supposed. He returned himself to active politics, and received in 1854 the post which had been withheld from him two years before. As President of the *Corps Législatif* he died in 1865. The disappearance of the Republic removed most of Flahault's scruples, the influence of the Emperor and of his own friends disposed of the rest. On December 31 he joined the Senate, where he soon became a constant attendant. Two years later he was appointed by Napoleon III. to the Commission which was charged with the publication of his uncle's correspondence—a task which appealed with special force to one who had himself been so near the person of the great Emperor. In 1860 he was offered and accepted the post of French Ambassador in London, while the year 1864 saw him installed as *Grand Chancelier* of the Legion of

Honour. Flahault breathed his last in Paris on
September the 1st, 1870, only a few hours before
the Second Empire received its death-blow at
Sedan.

INDEX

ABBATUCCI, Jacques Pierre Charles (1792–1857), a politician who early espoused the side of Louis Napoleon. He was appointed a member of the "Consultative Commission" after the *coup d'état*, and on Jan. 22, 1852, succeeded Rouher as Minister of Justice: 237, 308

ABDUL-MEDJID, Sultan of Turkey; succeeded his father, Mahomet VI., in 1839 and died in 1861: 103, 329

ABERDEEN, George Gordon, 4th Earl of (1784–1860), Prime Minister in 1852 after Lord Derby's resignation: 127, 334, 335

ALBEMARLE, George Thomas Keppel, 6th Earl of (1799–1891), General; groom-in-waiting to the Queen and some time member of Parliament: 213

ALBERT OF SAXE-COBURG, Prince, the Prince Consort (1819–1861): 66, 141, 146, 239, 301

D'ALBUFÉRA, Madame (1791–1844), the widow of Suchet, Duc d'Albuféra, who had died in 1826, and daughter of Baron de St. Joseph, Mayor of Marseilles; was distantly connected with the Bonaparte family: 207

ANONYMOUS letter to Flahault: 312

ANSON, Hon. Mrs. Isabella, daughter of the 1st Lord Forester, and one of five sisters all noted for their beauty. She married in 1830 the Hon. George Anson, brother to the Earl of Lichfield, some time M.P. and afterwards Commander-in-Chief in India: 144

ARTAUD, Mme., a *femme de charge* employed by Prince Metternich; she had formerly been in the service of Lady Jersey: 102

ASHLEY, Lord (1801–1885), Anthony Ashley Cooper, the eminent philanthropist, better known as Lord Shaftesbury, which he became on the death of his father in June, 1851. He married in 1830 Emily, daughter of 5th Earl Cowper: 141, 143

D'AUDENARDE, Mme., the wife of Vicomte d'Audenarde, who had been equerry to the Emperor Napoleon: 107

D'AUMALE, Henri Eugène Philippe Louis d'Orléans, Duc (1822–1897), fourth son of King Louis Philippe. After his father's abdication he lived in England, where he produced some incisive pamphlets against Louis Napoleon: 190

AUPICK, Jacques (1789–1857), French General; appointed Ambassador at Constantinople by the Republican Government in 1848, but three years later he exchanged this post for that of Madrid: 103

343

INDEX

BACCIOCHI, Félix, Comte, the
nephew and heir of Bacciochi,
Prince de Lucques, who mar-
ried Napoleon's sister Eliza.
During the Second Empire
Comte Bacciochi was appointed
premier chambellan to Napoleon
III.; died 1866: 259

BALMAIN, Alexandre, Comte de, a
Russian who represented his
country as Commissioner at
St. Helena, during Napoleon's
captivity on that island: 64

BARAGUAY D'HILLIERS, Achille,
Comte (1795–1878), General
and afterwards a Marshal of
France. He replaced General
Changarnier as Commandant
of the army of Paris in Jan.,
1851, and later distinguished
himself in the wars against
Russia and Italy: 145

BARROT, Camille Hyacinthe Odilon
(1791–1873), a Liberal statesman and orator. He was the
head of Louis Napoleon's first
Ministry, but fell out of the
President's favour, and was
amongst the 200 deputies arrested at the time of the *coup
d'état:* 110, 148, 177

BARTHÉLEMY, Marquis de, a
prominent member of the
Royalist party and secretary
of the committee whose headquarters were in the Rue St.
Florentin. He was the signa-
tory of a document which,
though intended only for private circulation, fell into the
hands of the press in September, 1850: 123

BATHYANY, Comtesse, married
Alexandre de Lutheroth, who
served for some time in the
French diplomatic service: 160

BAUFFREMONT, (?) Alphonse, Duc
de (1792–1860), some time
aide-de-camp to Murat. He
became a senator in 1851: 108,
132

BAUFFREMONT (*fils*), son to the
preceding and married to a
Mlle. Leroux: 108

BAZE, Jean Didier (1800–1881),
one of the *Questeurs* of the
Assembly. Having been ar-
rested on Dec. 2, 1851, he
refused to accept a pardon
and lived abroad till a general
amnesty was proclaimed in
1859: 194

BEAUMONT DE LA BONNINIÈRE,
Gustave Auguste de (1802–
1866), a moderate republican
whom Cavaignac had appointed
Ambassador in London in 1848.
The following year he was sent
in the same capacity to Vienna.
He was amongst those arrested
at the time of the *coup d'état*,
and thenceforward took no part
in public affairs: 102

BEAUVALE, Lord, Frederic James
Lamb (1782–1853), third son
of the 1st Viscount Melbourne.
After holding a number of high
diplomatic appointments, including the British ambassadorship at Vienna (where he
preceded Flahault), he was, in
1839, created Baron Beauvale.
In 1848 he succeeded his father
as Lord Melbourne: 267

BECK, Mme. de, 160

BEDEAU, Marie Alphonse (1804–
1863), General. He was Vice-
President of the *Assemblée
Constituante* and of the *Assemblée Législative*. Arrested and
exiled in Dec., 1851, he did not
return to France till the general
amnesty was proclaimed in
1859: 207, 262

BEDFORD, Francis Russell, 7th
Duke of (1788–1862): 57

BELLOCQ, (?) Le chevalier Bellocq,
some time in the French diplomatic service: 108

BEM, Joseph (1795–1850), Polish
General, who had lived much
in Paris. He was actively concerned in the Austrian revolution of 1848; after its repression
he fled to Turkey and became a
Mahomedan: 103, 104, 105

BERRYER, Antoine Pierre (1790–
1868), advocate and orator. A

344

INDEX

BERRYER, Antoine Pierre—*Con.* protagonist of the Legitimist party. He was elected a member of the Academy in 1852: 177, 195, 298

BERTHIER, Alexandre, Prince de Neufchâtel and Wagram (1753–1815), the companion of Napoleon in all his expeditions; Marshal of France: 53

BINEAU, appointed Minister of Finance on Jan. 22, 1852, in the place of Fould, who had resigned on the *Confiscation* decree: 237

BOIGNE, Adèle, Comtesse de, daughter of the Marquis d'Osmond, authoress of *Une Passion dans le grand monde* and the well-known *Mémoires:* 58, 59

BOILAY, Antoine Fortuné (1802–1866), was employed on the staff of the *Constitutionnel* newspaper from 1848 till 1851, when he received the appointment of *Secrétaire Général* to the Council of State: 155

BONAPARTE, Maria Letitia, the wife of a Corsican officer and mother of the Emperor Napoleon. She died in 1836: 92

BONAPARTE, Louis (1778–1846), younger brother of Napoleon, who instituted him King of Belgium in 1806. He married Hortense Beauharnais in 1802, but separated from her six years later: 53, 92, 316

BONAPARTE, Hortense Eugénie (1783–1837), daughter of the Empress Josephine by her first husband Viscount Beauharnais and wife of Louis, King of Holland, mother of Louis Napoleon and of Morny. She separated from her husband in 1807, and after the fall of Napoleon lived abroad under the name of the Duchesse de St. Leu: *55, et seq.,* 91, 127, 143

BONAPARTE, Jérôme (1784–1860), youngest brother of Napoleon; some time King of Westphalia.

Having lived out of France for many years, he was, in 1848, made Governor of the *Invalides;* two years later he became a Marshal. By his second wife, Princess Catherine of Wurtemburg, he was the father of Princess Mathilde and of Napoleon Joseph Charles, better known as "Plon-Plon": 90, 110, 313

BOTHMER, Count, of Bothmer, Mecklenburg-Schwerin, and of King George III.'s German Legion: 63

BOWOOD, near Calne in Wiltshire, the residence of the Marquis of Lansdowne: 153, 206, 211, 239, 241

BROCKET HALL, Hertfordshire, the residence of the 1st Lord Melbourne. It passed on the death of the 1st Lord to his son, better known as Lord Beauvale, and from him (in 1853) to his sister Lady Palmerston: 267

BROGLIE, Achille Charles Léonce Victor, Duc de (1785–1870), Foreign Secretary and Prime Minister under Louis Philippe. Under the Presidency he worked for a constitutional solution of the many questions which arose between Louis Napoleon and the Assembly. After 1851 he lived in retirement: 110, 139, 166, 174, 184, 191

BRUCE, Lady Mary Caroline Herbert, daughter of Lord Pembroke and wife of George, Lord Bruce, who in 1856 succeeded his father as 2nd Marquis of Ailesbury: 156

BUGEAUD, Thomas (1784–1849). During the reign of Louis Philippe he served with distinction in Algeria and Morocco, and gained the title of Duc d'Isly. He died of cholera in Paris: 88

BYRON, George Gordon, Lord (1788–1824), the famous poet: 64

345

INDEX

CANNING, Stratford, 1st Viscount Stratford de Redcliffe (1786–1880), diplomatist, Ambassador from 1842 till 1858 at Constantinople, where his policy was directed towards the maintenance of the integrity of the Ottoman Empire: 103

CANOUVILLE, an officer at one time prominent at the Court of the First Empire and an early friend of Flahault: 207

CARAMAN, Mme. de, the widow of Victor Marie Joseph Louis de Riquet, Marquis de Caraman (died 1837), who had been aide-de-camp to Napoleon I. with Flahault during the First Empire: 139

CARBONEL, a nephew of the Carbonel who was some time *maître de harpe* to Queen Hortense. He was aide-de-camp to Flahault during the final stages of the First Empire, and later (under Louis Philippe) held the post of Chief of the Staff in the *Garde Nationale:* 107, 139

CARLISLE, George William Howard, 7th Earl of (1802–1864), some time a member of Parliament, Chancellor of the Duchy of Lancaster in Lord John Russell's Government, 1849–1851; afterwards Lord-Lieutenant of Ireland: 105

CARNOT, Lazare Hippolyte (1801–1888), a son of the great Carnot and father of the President. He had supported the revolutionary movement in 1848, and though he failed at the time to secure re-election, he was returned (with Flotte and Vidal) at the by-elections held in Paris in May, 1851. He actively opposed the *coup d'état*, but he was not amongst those who were proscribed: 117

CASABIANCA, François Xavier, Comte de (1796–1881), a politician of Corsican extraction, who attached himself to the Prince-President. He became successively Minister of Agri-culture and of Finance, and after the *coup d'état* was entrusted with the formation of a new Ministry of State, inaugurated by the Presidential decree of Jan. 22, 1852: 277

CASSAGNAC, Adolphe Granier de (1806–1880), journalist. He started as a supporter of the Orleanist cause but transferred his affections to the Prince-President. He was editor of a semi-official paper called *Le Pays:* 123, 164

CAVAIGNAC, Louis Eugène (1802–1857), gained great distinction as a soldier in Algeria during the reign of Louis Philippe. Called to Paris as Minister of War in 1848, and quelled in four days the formidable insurrection which took place in June of that year. As official Republican candidate for the Presidency he received only 1,500,000 votes against 5,-500,000 cast for Louis Napoleon. He married in 1851 a Mlle. Odier: 78, *et seq.*, 80, 101, 127, 139, 157, 184, 205, 208 *et seq.*

CHABANNES LA PALICE, Alfred Jean Eginhard, Comte de (b. 1799), had been aide-de-camp to King Louis Philippe and followed him into exile. He remained with the ex-Queen Amélie till her death: 102

CHAMBORD, Henri Charles Dieudonné, Duc de Bordeaux and Comte de (1820–1883), posthumous son of the Duc de Berri. He was the "Legitimist" heir to the French throne, in succession to his grandfather Charles X., the Comte de Paris, grandson of Louis Philippe, being the representative of the younger or "Orleanist" branch of the Bourbon family. During the Second Republic "Henry V." was living at Frohsdorf in Lower Austria, where he eventually died without successor: 111, 123, 138, 210

346

INDEX

347

INDEX

INDEX

FLAHAULT, Margaret Mercer, Comtesse de (1788–1867), daughter of Lord Keith and Jane Mercer (grand-daughter of Robert Nairne, who had married the heiress of the Mercers of Aldie). She became in her own right (1) Baroness Keith, in succession to her father; (2) Baroness Nairne, on the extinction of the elder branch of that family by the death of William, the 4th Lord Nairne, in 1837: *see* Introduction, etc.
Letter from: 129

FLAHAULT, Emily de: see Shelburne, Lady

FLAHAULT, Georgine de (1822–1907), third daughter of the Flahaults; married Félix, Marquis de Lavalette, soon after her father's death in 1870: 64, 105, 107, 135, 163, 188, 307

FLAHAULT, Louise de, youngest daughter of the Flahaults (b. 1825). She suffered from consumption and died in 1853 at the age of eighteen: 64, 174, 186, 187, 200, 335

FLOCON, Ferdinand (1800–1866), a journalist who identified himself with the extreme Republican party at the Revolution of 1848, and after being Secretary to the Provisional Government became for a time one of its members. He was banished in Dec., 1851: 88

FLORENTON, Queen Hortense's coachman. In 1851 he was in the service of Prince Louis Napoleon: 143

FOREY, Elie Frédéric (1804–1872), *Général de Brigade* and an ardent partisan of Louis Napoleon. As such he was instrumental in the military measures taken in Paris on Dec. 4, 1851, and subsequently took an active part in the wars of the Second Empire. A Marshal of France: 177

FORTUNATO, Minister of the Neapolitan Government in 1849: 104

FOUCHÉ, Joseph (1763–1820), Duke of Otranto. He was head of the Police under Napoleon, and held the same post at the commencement of the reign of Louis XVIII.: 56

FOULD, Achille (1800–1867), financier and politician. Four times Minister of Finance under Louis Napoleon's presidency. He resigned on the question of the Confiscation of the Orleans property, but subsequently became Senator and Minister of State: 177, 191, 237, 254, *et seq.*, 267, 277 *et seq.*

FROHSDORF, near Wiesbaden, in Lower Austria, where the Comte de Chambord (the "Henry V." of the "Legitimist" party) lived during and after the Presidency of Louis Napoleon: 123

FURSTENBURG, Charles Egon, Prince de (1796–1854), a German who took service first in Austria and afterwards in Baden, where in 1818 he married Amélie, the daughter of the Grand Duke Charles Frédéric: 144

GERVAIS DE CAEN (1803–1867), a doctor born at Caen who became Prefect of Police for a short time in 1848. He was afterwards associated with commerce rather than with politics: 85

GIRARDIN, Alexandre Louis Robert, Comte de (1776–1855), an early friend of Flahault's. They served together under Napoleon and became Generals about the same time: 210

GIRARDIN, Mme. de, *née* Mlle. Fagnan, the wife of Count Alexandre de Girardin, whom she had married in 1810: 139, 210

GLADSTONE, William Ewart (1809–1898). During Louis Napoleon's Presidency he was in the "Peelite" group of the House

350

INDEX

INDEX

INDEX

MARBEUF, Louis Charles René, Comte de (1712–1786), the French General who, in 1769, became Military Governor of Corsica. He befriended the Bonaparte family, and procured for the young Napoleon the advantages of a French education: 92, 94

MARIE AMÉLIE DE BOURBON, Queen, Queen of the French, wife of King Louis Philippe, whom she married in 1809; daughter of Ferdinand IV., King of the Two Sicilies; died at Claremont in 1866, 136, 164, 262, 264
Letter from Flahault to, 248

MASSA, Mme. de: see Roger, Baronne de

MATHILDE, Princess, Mathilde Letitia Wilhelmine Bonaparte (1820–1904), daughter of Jérôme Bonaparte, Napoleon's youngest brother. She married in 1840 the Russian Prince, Anatole Demidoff, but separated from him a few years afterwards. She usually did the honours of the Elysée for her cousin the Prince-President; after his marriage this building was given to her as a residence: 91, 110, 144, 146, 160, 165

MAUPAS, Charlemagne Emile de (1818–1888), held some minor appointments during the earlier years of the Presidency, and in Oct., 1851, became Prefect of Police. On Jan. 22, 1852, he was made Minister of Police, and later on he accepted a seat on the Senate. His *Mémoires sur le Second Empire* were published in 1884–1885: 151, 173, 219, 236, 237, 252, 255, *et seq.*, 277, 280, 313 *et seq.*
Report on the Casualties of the *coup d'état*, 219

MAUSSION, 156

MEATH, William Brabazon, 11th Earl of (1803–1887), 214

MERCER, Jane, eldest daughter and heiress of Colonel William Mercer of Aldie and Meikleour in Perthshire. She married George Keith Elphinstone (afterwards Viscount Keith) in 1787, and died leaving an only daughter (afterwards Madame de Flahault) in 1789: 58, 62

MÉRODE, Charles Werner Ghislain, Comte de (1816–1905), a member of the Assembly who acted throughout with the party of reaction and supported the *coup d'état.* He was brother-in-law to Montalembert: 189, 194

METTERNICH, Clement, Prince de (1773–1859), Chancellor of State of the Austrian Empire for nearly forty years. After the Revolution of 1848 he made his escape from Vienna and came to England. In 1849 he established himself at Brussels and in 1851 at Johannesburg, whence he returned soon afterwards to Vienna. He was three times married: 105

METTERNICH, Princesse de, Comtesse Mélanie Zichy-Ferraris (1805–1854), third wife of Prince Metternich, whom she married in 1831: 102

METTERNICH-WINNEBURG, Prince Richard de (1829–1895), eldest son of the great Prince Metternich by his second wife, the Baroness Leykarn. He entered the diplomatic service and eventually became Ambassador at Paris. In 1856 he married Pauline Sandor: 102, 139

METTERNICH-WINNEBURG, Hermione de, a daughter of Metternich by his first marriage: 105

METTERNICH-WINNEBURG, Mélanie de (b. 1832), daughter of Prince Metternich by his third wife, the Comtesse Zichy-Ferraris. She afterwards married Comte Zichy de Vasony-kaia: 105

DE MEYNARD, a lawyer who (with Troplong and Rouher) was much consulted by Louis Na-

355

INDEX

INDEX

PACHA, the, of Egypt, Abbas
Pacha, who had succeeded to
the post of hereditary Viceroy
of Egypt on the death of
Ibrahim Pacha in 1848: 329

PACIFICO, David (1784–1854),
known as "Don Pacifico," a
Portuguese adventurer who, in
1850, had a quarrel with the
Greek Government. Palmerston's support of his claims
caused a temporary ministerial
crisis: 117

PALMERSTON, Henry John Temple,
3rd Viscount (1784–1865),
Prime Minister, etc. He was
Foreign Secretary under Lord
John Russell, 1846 to 1851:
72, 104, 121, 127, 154, 155,
196–9, 202–3, 211, et seq.,
228, et seq., 237, 242, 244, 291,
306
Letter from, 231
Flahault's conversation with, 296

PALMERSTON, Lady Emily Mary
Lamb, daughter of 1st Lord
Melbourne. She married 1st
(1805) the 5th Earl Cowper,
and 2nd (1839), Henry John
Temple, Viscount Palmerston.
She inherited Brocket from her
father: 148, 241
Letters from, 241, 277

PANSHANGER, in Hertfordshire,
the residence of George, 6th
Earl Cowper, whose mother
had married Lord Palmerston:
162, 193

PARIS, Louis Philippe Albert
d'Orléans, Comte de (1838–
1894), grandson of King Louis
Philippe. On the death of his
father, the Duc d'Orléans, in
1842, he became head of the
Orleanist dynasty: 97, 136, 211

PASQUIER, Etienne Denis, Duc de
(1767–1862). He served successively under Napoleon, the
Bourbons, and Louis Philippe,
but took no part in politics
after 1848: 129, 194

PASSY, a suburb of Paris near the
Bois de Boulogne where Flahault's friends, the Delesserts,
were living at the time of the
coup d'état: 106, 139, 143, 163,
187

PEMBROKE, Robert Henry Herbert, 12th Earl of (1791–
1862), died s.p. and was succeeded by his nephew: 144

PEMBROKE, Lady, Princess Octavia Spinelli, daughter of the
Duke of Laurino and widow of
the Sicilian Prince Buttera de
Rubari. She married (2nd) in
1814 Robert Herbert, 12th Earl
of Pembroke, and died in 1857:
156

PERSIGNY, Jean Gilbert Victor
Fialin, Duc de (1808–1872), the
principal supporter of Louis
Napoleon in the affairs of Strasburg (1836) and Boulogne
(1840). He soon became prominent during the Presidency,
and was made Minister of the
Interior in succession to Morny
in 1852. From 1855 to 1860 he
was Ambassador to England:
151, 173, 201, 235, 237, 255, 256,
257, 258, et seq., 277, 285, 307
Letter from, 195

PISCATORY, Théobald Emile Arcambal (1799–1870), politician
and diplomat under Louis
Philippe. He retired for a
time after the Revolution, but
was elected to the Assembly in
1849, and joined the antirevolutionary party, though he
did not support the coup d'état:
177, 207, 252

PRASLIN, Duchesse de, Fanny,
daughter of the Napoleonic
General, Sébastiani, and the
wife of the Duc de Choiseul
Praslin. In 1847 Madame de
Praslin was found dead in her
room, and shortly afterwards
her husband (who was suspected of the murder) committed suicide. L'affaire Praslin was said to have been the
outcome of an intrigue of the
Duke's with his children's governess, which had become
known to his wife: 165

358

INDEX

SAINTE-AULAIRE, Louis—*Con.*
Napoleon, but later became a
politician and a diplomat, eventually retiring from public life
in 1848. He was the author
of several historical works:
140

SALIGNY, 252

SALVANDY, Narcisse Achille,
Comte de (1795–1856), twice
Minister for Public Instruction under Louis Philippe:
123

SANDOR, Pauline (b. 1836). The
daughter of Comte Sandor and
of Metternich's eldest daughter
by his first wife. In 1856 she
married Richard Metternich,
the Chancellor's son by his
second wife; she was a prominent figure at the Court of the
Second Empire: 105

SANDWICH, Lady, Louisa Corry,
daughter of the 1st Earl of
Belmore, and widow of George
John, 6th Earl of Sandwich.
Her daughter Catherine was
the first wife of Count Walewski: 139

SAUX, M. de, a gentleman through
whom Flahault communicated
with the *Morning Post*, 239:
246

SÉGUR, Philippe Paul, Comte de
Ségur (1780–1873), General and
historian; took no part in political affairs 1848–1852: 194,
207

SHELBURNE, Henry Petty-Fitz-
maurice, Earl of (1816–1866),
eldest surviving son of the 3rd
Lord Lansdowne, whom he
succeeded as 4th Marquis in
1863. M.P. for Colne from
1847 to 1856; afterwards Under-
Secretary for Foreign Affairs:
65, 266

SHELBURNE, Lady, Emily Jane
Mercer Elphinstone de Flahault (1819–1895), eldest
daughter and heiress of the
Comte and Comtesse de Flahault; married in 1842, as his
second wife, Henry, Earl of

Shelburne (4th Marquis of
Lansdowne); she was the mother of the present Lord Lansdowne: 65, 99, 139, 151, 155,
163, 186, 194, 248, 333
Letters from, 156, 157, 162, 263,
266

SHERIDAN, Richard Brinsley (1751–
1816), dramatist, 300

SMALL, M., 252

SOULT, Nicolas Jean de Dieu
(1769–1851), the celebrated
French Marshal. He died on
Nov. 26, 1851: 326

SOUZA-BOTELHO, José Maria, Marquis de (1758–1825). He was
some time Portuguese Am-
bassador in Paris, where he
married Madame de Flahault
in 1802. He edited the *Lusiades*
of the famous poet Camoëns:
52, 67

SOUZA, Madame de (1761–1836),
née Adèle Filleul. Married (1st)
in 1779 Charles François,
Comte de Flahault. He was
guillotined in 1793. She married (2nd) in 1802 Don José
Maria de Souza-Botelho: 28 *et
seq.*, 65, 68

STANLEY, Mrs. John; Marie, the
only daughter of Baron de
Talleyrand and wife of John
Massey Stanley, who later
(1876), on the death of his elder
brother, became Sir John Stanley Errington. Mrs. John
Stanley was a very beautiful
woman, and a close friend of
the Empress Eugénie. She died
about 1910: 114

STÉPHANIE DE BADE, Grand
Duchess, daughter of Count
Claude de Beauharnais and
niece of Alexandre de Beauharnais, the first husband of
the Empress Josephine. She
married Charles Louis Frede-
rick, Grand Duke of Baden,
and was the mother of Lady
Douglas: 115, 117

STOCKHAUSEN (?), General Baron
de (1791–1861). He was Minister for War in Prussia: 160

360

INDEX

361

INDEX